What makes
Tough guys tough?

The Secret Domain
By

Jamie O'Keefe

Published by New Breed publishing

Printed by

New Breed Publishing
PO BOX 2676, ROMFORD, ESSEX RM7 0LP

www.newbreedbooks.co.uk

Reprinted in April 2004 (8th edition)

A CIP catalogue record for this book is available from the British Library

Printed and bound in Great Britain.

ISBN 0 9517567 2 9

Please note: The theoretical information and physical techniques outlined in this book are for self-protection and Self-defence purposes only. The author and the publishers cannot accept any responsibility for any proceedings or prosecutions brought or instituted against any person or body as a result of the misuse of any theoretical information or physical techniques described in this book or any loss, injury or damage caused thereby.

Dedicated to all the true tough guys
that have no need prove themselves

Acknowledgements

Thanks to:-

Geoff Thompson, Peter Consterdine, Dave Turton, Bob Sykes, Dave 'Boy' Green, Mo Hussein, Buddie C, Micky Byrne, Richy Horsley, Roy 'Pretty Boy' Shaw and Kevin Fox for allowing me to interview them for this book, also for allowing me to use photographs from their own personal collections.

Front cover photo: *Dave 'Boy' Green*

Contents

Contents

FOREWORD
BY
DAVID TURTON 8th DAN GOSHINKWAI COMBAT
Chief Instructor - Self Defence Federation

When I was asked by Jamie to write a foreword to this, his latest book, I was both pleased & honoured, and a little intimidated by the prospect.

The first seemingly obvious thing I did, was to read it..

Sounds obvious, but I mean **REALLY** read. On doing so, I found myself being drawn quite deeply into Jamie's thoughts and ideals.

Jamie tends to venture into fields that few, if any, other authors have entered. In doing so, he lays open many often-unanswered questions. He makes those of you-who have asked themselves these soul searching questions, feel that they are not alone.

Having known Jamie for more years than both of us care to remember, I have the advantage of being able to 'hear' his voice, whilst reading his words. I can hear the inflections that show his passion in his beliefs, and the sheer sense of honesty of his words.

Read this book with no other distractions, and give it the respect of doing so with your full attention. Only then the effort will be rewarded with the insight you will get.

I first met Jamie 0'Keefe around twenty years ago. I was a Guest Instructor on an All-Styles self-defence course, and Jamie was a participant on the course, a very noticeable one at that.

I thought here was a talented Karate-Ka, a bit brash, but Oh, so very eager to learn. He was mainly into what we thought of as 'Free-style' Karate back then, but searching for something more. His thirst for learning was nearly insatiable. His Black Belt status was of no real consequence to him. He simply wanted to get stuck in and learn.

He's still doing just that. ... **THE SAME ENTHUSIASM IS PARAMOUNT IN HIS WRITINGS.**

I have looked for a way to go past the usual platitudes, and try to give; what I feel is an honest appraisal of what I feel Jamie is trying to give.... Then it registered ... That's the word ... **HONEST**.. That's the man and his writings.

Jamie always 'tells it like it is'. No holds barred, and no respecter of the many fragile Egos so prevalent in the Martial Arts these days. In this, he ranks along my two other favourite HONEST Combat Authors ... Geoff Thompson and Peter Consterdine.

Don't read this book for 'ways to do it', Don't read this book and be offended by his honesty. Read it, because NOT to read it, will leave a massive hole in your understandings of the World of Man & Violence.

Make it part of your collection, but keep going back to it to read it again and again.

I RECOMMEND THIS BOOK,
I DON'T RECOMMEND MANY... '**READ IT**'

DAVID TURTON 8th DAN GOSHINKWAI COMBAT.
Chief Instructor – The Self Defence Federation

Introduction

Firstly, thank you for taking the time to read this book on the subject of what makes tough guys tough. Full apologies to the females out there for my choosing of a title and theme that could be regarded as a touch sexist, however it is certainly not meant to be. I just thought it was a great title to choose and use. I did in fact spend two years of my life writing my first ever book just for the ladies called 'Dog's don't know kung fu' the female guide to self-protection which I think balances the scales a little.

As for this book - why have I written a book on the subject of what makes tough guys tough?

Is it because I'm a tough guy, a boxing champ, a bodyguard, a soldier of fortune? Sorry-but no. I am none of these. So why did I choose to write a book about something that I have never been?

Well simply because it hasn't been done before and people like you desire to read books like this, and most importantly, we all secretly want to know 'what makes tough guys tough.' This book was published years before the current phase of 'Hard Bastard' type books and if you look closely enough you will see similar attributes in many of the books that followed this one.

At some time in all our lives we have desired to be a little tougher than we currently felt we were in order to deal with certain situations that have made us feel vulnerable and weak. We have all wondered why we cannot be as tough as someone that we know of. We have all admired the movie screen hero or heroine that has overcome weakness to suddenly save the day by becoming tougher than they were previously thought to be.

Its an area that we are constantly dealing with in all walks of life, yet we still do not know what it is that makes someone tough. What is it that makes one person tough but another not!

I decided to research this subject and explore the whole concept of toughness in order to help discover the answer to what makes tough people tough.

There were literally hundreds of people I wanted to interview and also some pretty heavyweight individuals that expressed a desire to be in this book, who all have been rejected for a number of reasons.

Some were pure thugs or wannabe thugs, some were heavy into villainy or again wannabees, and others were plain bullshitters.

In the end I decided to only use people that had **NOT** requested me to use them in my book. In other words, people that I would have paid to interview if I had to, people that I personally have bundles of respect for, and most important of all – people that I believe are giving truthful and honest answers straight from the heart and were not bothered whether they appeared in this book or not.

There are a few other faces that I would like to have included within this book like Reggie Kray, Lenny McLean, etc. but due to time restraints and restrictions imposed by HM Prison with Reg at my time of interviewing him and the sudden loss of Lenny, along with other projects that other known characters were committed to at the time of writing, it has not been possible to include everyone I wanted to..

I truly hope that this book inspires you to look at yourself and any areas of your life that are likely to be changed in any way when it comes down to personal toughness. Also if you are within any training discipline for the purpose of becoming tougher, I hope this book will offer you a more informed choice as to whether you are treading along the most suitable path – for your desired outcome. If this book makes you think about toughness from another perspective or helps you to understand the undiscovered area, and secret domain of what makes tough guys tough – my writing and your reading has all been worthwhile. If possible, it would be great if you could go direct to the questionnaire 'Your chance to answer' on pages 150 so that you can answer the questions about toughness without influence from this book. Then answer the same questions after reading this book to see if any of your views have changed.

I hope you enjoy this book and go on to read my other books.

Jamie O'Keefe   6th Dan (F.S.M.A.)
Founder Fellow of the Society of Martial Arts
And definitely not a tough guy…

The Secret Domain

What do we mean by tough?

This meat is a bit tough!
How to approach this problem- that's a tough one!
Tough luck!
I hear you're a tough guy?
Don't mess with him, he's a tough guy!
If you don't like what I have to say - that's tough!

What do we really mean by the word tough? Isolating the word and defining exactly what we mean is not an easy one.

Philosophers have for centuries been trying to find out what we mean when using words or concepts.
So for the purpose of this book I will begin by placing an image in your head.

Society associates and attaches the label of 'Tough' to certain real life and fictional characters like Rambo, Conan, Rocky, Action man, Popeye, and so on.

Let's look at this, as the area of understanding that we are associating the word tough with, for the purpose of having a starting point from which to explore 'What makes tough guys tough.'

Now I must make you TOUGH!

We are what we learn

We are what we learn.

It matters a great deal as to how we learn because the way we learn, affects the final outcome of what we become. Let's identify the principles of learning. The learning domains.

The three areas of learning, or the three ways in which we learn are:

1. Psychomotor Learning
2. Cognitive Learning
3. **Affective Learning**

I will break these areas down so that you can look at them more clearly.

Psychomotor learning

Psychomotor: of or relating to movement or muscular activity associated with mental processes.

Psychomotor is also referred to as Motor Fitness. It is composed of SPEED - BALANCE- CO-ORDINATION.

To give an easier visualisation of Motor Fitness, I will use an common recognisable example of 'what it is like when we lose these abilities.'

Take a look at someone who is drunk or under the influence of alcohol. The smallest amount of alcohol will take its toll on our motor fitness. At least one of the components of Motor fitness, if not all of them, will begin to deteriorate.

Speech is one of the most noticeable of effects of alcohol in our body. The co-ordination of our lip and tongue, working in time with out vocal side, becomes a real task.

Add to this our sad attempt to walk to the bar or toilet, trying to disguise the fact that we are wobbling un-controllably and our body slows down rapidly! In fact, we end up so slow that we come to a stop.

I hope this explains some of the effects of loss or deterioration of Motor fitness ability, or at least makes it easier to understand.

I will now focus on the enchantment of our Motor fitness abilities.

A good example to use and one that we are all aware of is the Juggler. What a fine example of Speed-Balance & Co-ordination all working in harmony with each other, demonstrating good Motor fitness ability.

Most of us fit somewhere in-between the Drunk and the Juggler.

If we want to learn a Martial art, bike riding, Gymnastics etc. We have to learn how to do this type of body movement.

Some Motor fitness abilities naturally cross over into other areas, making Psychomotor learning easy.

Me in training with Cass Magda & Danny Inosanto - mid 80s

For example, if you learn one Style of Kick-Punch martial art, you would normally find it easier to cross over into another Kick-Punch style of martial art.

This is because your body already has its main core of Motor fitness abilities & skills from which to draw from. So moving from one style of Karate to another is relatively a straightforward process.

However moving from Karate to Judo, or Aikido to Boxing, is a different matter altogether because the difference in Psychomotor skills, ability and performance is far different and do not naturally cross over.

Me and Bob Breen at my Full time studio 'The New Breed Academy' Walthamstow East London 1987

They do not have many matching attributes, if any at all.
They are as different as Chess and Draughts or Judo and Wrestling.

When you go to a club that's teaching a Martial art or fighting related system, the main and **<u>sometimes only</u>** area of learning that you will encounter, is Psychomotor learning.

It is this area that we see and are most impressed with when first exposed to the fighting arts, but sadly, 99% of our time is spent in this area which will undoubtedly enhance our Motor fitness ability, but will never make us 'Hard or tough.'

What it can do, is fine tune and turn tough guys into precision fighting machines. Boxers are a prime example of this - Softies do not last in Boxing.

Psychomotor/Motor fitness is a must in all-fighting arts, but it will never make you a tough guy!

'Footballers strive to sharpen their psychomotor abilities
but some do think that being a tough guy is also
an important part of the art.'

Cognitive learning

Cognitive: The mental process or faculty of knowing.
In simple terms, this is where you use your brain for Problem Solving, remembering things, recalling information and facts etc. Martial art systems use this area to learn and remember correct sequences or patterns of movement. Whether or not their psychomotor ability is technically correct-it does not matter, it's the brains thought process that will take them through the correct pattern of movements.

This area allows us to visualise our movements, over and over again, even whilst relaxing in the bath.
Dancers, Gymnasts, actors, all use cognitive learning as an important part of their desired end result.

Don't make the mistake though of always connecting Motor fitness automatically with Cognitive learning ability.

Great Chess players rely tremendously on their Cognitive learning & problem solving with virtually no Psychomotor/Motor fitness application, except for physically lifting a chess piece up, then putting it back down onto another square. You could say that the Psychomotor learning process for the Chess player & Draughts player would be the same for the purpose of playing their individual games, but their

Cognitive learning, problem solving, and application of knowledge are vastly different.

Chess is a mind game played between two opposing sides with three possible results: You win - You lose - or You draw.

My children studying the cognitive 'Art of War'

I taught my children to play Chess at a very young age for the very purpose of introducing them to problem solving and looking at situations from many angles. Chess, problem solving, draws greatly from Awareness-Evaluation & Avoidance, which I believe, sets as a level for problem solving throughout your life.

When I taught Self-protection to former World Boxing Champion Terry Marsh. He was always able to apply problem solving from a perspective that others would never consider approaching it from. It was nothing to do with his outstanding Boxing ability - but rather his cognitive learning and problem solving ability, which is not normally associated with Boxers.

I say this with no demeaning overtones with regards to the intelligence of boxers. They are a special breed that have the balls to get in there and 'do it' rather than just view it from a safe zone and criticise it like most other boxing experts. They have my utmost respect just for getting in there. As do Cage fighters, Judo players and all other physical contact artists.

Terry Marsh was a real intelligent individual who achieved his Black belt with me and could have made a big impact within the Martial arts world, but unfortunately, shortly after, he was accused of the shooting of Frank Warren, which he was later found, not guilty of.

Whilst in prison awaiting trial, he wrote to me saying that he was making good use of his time learning to speak another language and keeping his brain active. His cognitive learning and problem solving ability was

special.

How many other Boxers do you know who were also schoolboy chess champions like Marsh? I think Chess as a strong cognitive foundation has a lot to answer for!

In our exchange of - Words of wisdom – Terry wrote to me *'A quitter never wins and a winner never quits..'* At the time I was discussing the idea of maybe writing a book one-day. This is my third book in print and I have since released another three, giving me six released books in all!

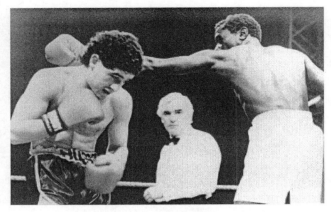

My good friend Mo Hussein in action

Terry Marsh is a good example of Cognitive learning and Psychomotor learning working in harmony with each other, but we must remember that the two do not always have to be connected.

My youngest son has enough basic knowledge to play chess but does so against a chess computer that uses no psychomotor movements whatsoever.

This is evidence that one area of learning can be without the other, along with its application. The chess computer uses only the cognitive problem solving area, even if it is only artificial intelligence.

In the fighting arts, it's the cognitive area that gives us the great masters, philosophers, teachers, and like, along with '**The art of fighting - without fighting**' quoted by the famous Bruce Lee.

Time and study gives these special individuals the underpinning knowledge that makes them special within their field.

These individuals are not regarded as special human beings because their kick, punch, throw etc is the best there has ever been within their art. Rather, it is their ability to apply their theoretical and underpinning knowledge in place of, or in addition to any psychomotor/Motor fitness application.

I am not saying that this group of specialists are not capable of the physical elements of their art because that is not the case. I am merely saying that most of them excel in bringing out hidden qualities in other people because of their cognitive ability.

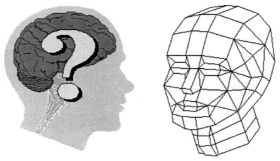

I always feel that when entering a fighting art gymnasium for the first time, you should not purely be in awe of the instructor and his abilities to perform the art in question. Rather, you should be in awe of the students that he or she has taught and transferred their knowledge to. It's knowledge that you are paying for. Good problem solving, cognitive ability makes tough guys clever.

But sadly, once again, I'm going to have to disappoint you. Cognitive learning does not make tough guys tough! However it will make their decision process work more from informed choice.

So if you are training hard on a regular basis and get the most from your Psychomotor learning, and also spend enough time absorbing knowledge, information, within your cognitive learning domain and still do not feel like a tough guy, where does the answer lie?

Well! I firmly believe that it is from the area which I term as 'The undiscovered area' or Secret domain, and that being

AFFECTIVE LEARNING…..

Affective learning

Affective: Influenced by or resulting from the emotions
What are the components of affective learning?
They are your

FEELINGS-ATTITUDE-EMOTIONS & VALUES.

For those of you who have skipped the sections on the Psychomotor and Cognitive learning domains, please go back and read them otherwise this Affective Learning area will not fit into place and may become meaningless.
Affective learning is definitely the undiscovered area!
I doubt if you have ever heard your Fighting arts teacher mention the term **affective learning**, let alone know anything about it.

You will have undoubtedly taken part in Psychomotor learning in any physical skill class that you join, and some instructors will partly try to teach you cognitive learning, even if they are not using this terminology, but none of them will touch on Affective learning. They don't understand that it's the important link to what makes tough guys tough.

So why is Affective learning so special?

Well as I said earlier, its about your feelings-attitude-emotions & values.
You can go to a class and learn how to move your body a certain way (Psychomotor) and even be taught how to think a certain way (Cognitive). Which you would do when performing a series of movements like combinations.
But is not really possible to truly teach you Attitude, Feelings, Emotions or values within a class.

You will be able to gain the odd experience here and there but the instant or long-term answer comes from life itself, over a period of time.

What you feel - is what you feel!

The affective learning domain that you have experienced has developed and nurtured from your days as an infant, right up to present day. It is our affective learning that makes us Hard, tough, introvert, extrovert, soft, shy, angry, racist, non-racist, sexist, and so on. In fact it really makes us what we are.

If you are at war with the world because you feel that you have had a raw deal in life, you feelings-attitude-emotions & values are likely to reflect this. You could come across as being very bitter towards people.

If you add to this bitterness, the brains thought process (Cognitive) and any physical capabilities; you could have an explosive nature ready to blow with the slightest of prompts. You could even end up a bully.

Not many people will recognise the fact that affective learning is a major contributor in turning out the end product, which could be an aggressive bully. All some will see, is that this person is supposedly 'Hard or tough.' What they are seeing is the psychomotor side only.

If a passive natured individual went to the same martial arts class as the bully, learnt the same psychomotor skills from that art, the same Cognitive learning and skills, you will end up with something quite different.

I've used the bully example here because it's easier to see and compare the same physical skills, because the bully will abuse his physical ability quite often.

Also its easier to see that if you took away the physical and cognitive ability from the bully, you will still have a bully, who is still as he is, because of his feelings-attitude and emotions which are imbedded into him, all part of his affective learning.

I will move away from the bully example onto another type of person who is 'hardened' because of their affective learning.

There are some people that have an Aura about them, which sends messages out telling others that they are not the type of person that you want to be messing with. Even without having seen them fight, or knowing anything of their reputation, you will still get that feeling.

It is quite evident that their psychomotor ability is an area that you can only speculate about, if you have never seen them perform. So all you are basing your views on is their problem solving ability-if any, along with the thing that is most evident, how they conduct themselves, which is an end product of their affective learning over the years.

Unlike the Psychomotor and Cognitive domains, Affective learning cannot be bottled and sold to you over the counter, or in the Martial arts gymnasium. We can go to any physical skill class to help us with the psychomotor domain. We can also go to 'Mensa' or similar IQ related organisations to work our cognitive domain, but where do you go to deal with our Feelings, attitude, emotions, and values?

You are the only person that has lived your life in the way you have experienced it. Nobody can change the past. You are what you are.

Putting a martial arts coloured belt around your waist, or punching a heavy bag, will not change that.

26

You can talk the talk all day long and speculate about what you will do in a confrontation, but when reality stares you in the face, you will feel - how you feel.

Terry Marsh in training at Ruskin Arms – East Ham, London

We can gear our training to get as close as possible to reality, **but only reality is reality**. Anything less than that is not real.

True real affective learning is the one ingredient that you cannot get by paying a weekly fee to your tutor. **Only time and experiences can give you affective learning**, be it good or bad. A lifetime of study gives us <u>life skills</u> and ability. These are too often overlooked.

If we could be graded on life skills and our ability to deal with confrontations, some of us would be 3rd, 4th & 5th Dan's in due to our theoretical & practical knowledge and ability within this field. Just have a think about how much knowledge of reality we really have?

It is so ignorant of us to judge a street fighter as having no grade and not knowing anything about the fighting arts, and automatically assuming that the Black belt is the be all, and end all, of the fighting arts.

If the street fighter was packaged and marketed, using the coloured belt system of the Martial arts. You would see a truer reflection of grades matching what they are currently thought to represent.

If you read my book **'Old School-New School'** which goes behind the scenes of ***Bouncers, Security and Registered Door Supervisors***, you will understand how the 'old school' bouncer operated and took care of business based on affective learning.

No hiding behind grades, no dry land swimming, they talked the talk as walked the walk.

This is then compared to the modern 'New school' door supervisor who is encouraged more to use problem solving in a defusing non psychomotor way.

They are becoming like the untested martial artist who uses his licence as an excuse to duck out of confrontations *'If I get in a fight, I will lose my licence.'*

In the martial arts the 'I will lose my licence' safety shield was used mainly by those that wanted to hide behind something. Door supervisors can genuinely make this claim because it is true and they can lose their licence. However the only ones that would ever consider pulling that line out of the hat are the ones that are really using their licence as a safety screen to avoid confrontation.

Don't misunderstand me though; I'm not saying that violence is the way. I'm merely highlighting how we act according to our affective learning. We are the end product of our upbringing.

Somebody who, for want of a better word, is a coward. Will still be that same coward even if you put a black belt around their waist or pin a Door supervisor's badge on their chest. They are what they are.

They might make all the right movements and think the right thoughts when theorising about what they will do when it kicks off, but nothing can change what they feel.

The only thing that the belt or badge may do is act as a safety barrier for a while which will enable the individual to explore and try out different ways of dealing with situations.

Gradually they can then start learning how things feel and may become desensitised to something that would normally frighten them.

There are no rules that say you cannot begin a different type of affective learning as from today.

It just becomes harder, the older you get, because once we reach adulthood we have pretty much made up our mind as to what we are prepared to accept regarding love, pain, fear, tolerance, and so on. We become set in our ways and do not want to stray too far outside our comfort zones.

Another thing that changes is our exposure to the possibility of confrontations.

A schoolboy is forced into a situation where literally hundreds of other boys will bump into him, make eye contact, compete against him, or may target him as the next victim.

The chances of any lad getting through school with out ever getting into a fight are pretty remote. I think that you time at school between 11-16 plays a major part in forming your character for the rest of your life.

As a child I was bullied continuously. If I carried on accepting the punishment without attempting to fight back, I would probably have seen the rest of my days withdrawn into a shell. Too frightened to even walk to the shops. There are people that live life like this.

At the schoolboy stage of my life my **feelings** **attitude** **emotions** & **values** were tearing me apart. My affective domain was beginning to structure me for the best or worst, depending on how I ended up as an adult.

My experiences cannot ever be felt by anybody else. They are unique to me and the only positive thing that I can draw from it is that I have made sure that my own children have never become victims.

Thinking about it, my whole career seems to be centered around dealing with the bully, be it as a doorman, a self protection instructor, or author of books advising people how to deal with confrontations.

For the sake of my children's future and how I raised them, I would not change my experiences. Other than that I would erase every day of my childhood out of my life.

However I cannot change my experiences and truly feel that my affective learning has made me succeed in my guise as a Self-protection instructor, doorman, blackbelt, etc etc.

If my life's experiences had taken a different route, I may still be in the guise connected to all these titles, but I might be more of a pretender who talks the talk but cannot walk the walk.

If the term 'Affective learning' clicked with you straight away, then you will probably be getting a little tired of me explaining it over and over again. However not everybody learns, absorbs or understands the same subject matter at the same rate.

For those people, which includes myself. I will give you another example of two people ending up quite different due to their affective learning, life's experiences and the all-important – learning environment...

Diary Entry

'Today I used my sisters home made dolls pram to carry all the junk, that we had put aside to sell down Brick Lane.
I had to get as much money as I could because we had no food indoors, no heating, no lights. My dad is on the run, in hiding from the police so is not able to provide for us. My mum is working as much as she can, but we still cannot survive after paying the rent man, provident and everything else we owe out. She is also still very ill.'

'One of the better off neighbours saw me and gave me three times what I had asked for an old ornament. I know they were being kind because they know how poor we are.
Later in the day the local gang passed by. They began the name calling and bad-mouthing my family. They all spat at me then ran off laughing. I wiped my face clean. I cried on the inside so no one could see.'

'I returned home with enough money to feed us and keep us warm until Friday, when my mother gets paid.
At school many of the kids are calling me 'Beggar boy' and teasing me, resulting in fights.'

'If it wasn't for the free school dinner, I would have skipped school, but I thought the more that I could eat at school, the less I would need at home. My mother was skipping meals to feed us. I would also get a bottle of milk in school.
Sometimes there were spares so I would pour them into a plastic bag and tie a knot to take it home.'

Excerpt taken from my diary as a schoolboy in the early 1970s. Whilst at the London Nautical Naval school.

Next follows a diary page from roughly the same time period in a child's life but within a far different Affective learning environment.
My eldest son wrote the following, aged 15 (now 22) in 1997. I asked him to describe a typical day from his life and to include some good and bad things that affect the way he feels in general.

'Today I went and got my monthly bus pass for school, My dad gave me £50 to cover my monthly fares and get a snack at dinner-times. Most of my mates get more than that. It's really embarrassing when I haven't got enough money to hire out a video or go to the pictures.

I know I've got cable with all the film channels, but I want to see the latest films out. Still at least I saw 'Eraser' a year before all

31

my mates did. My dad took me to see it when he took me to Disneyworld in Florida. He said we could go again when he can afford it. He took the whole family to Butlins for two weeks recently but I didn't bother going.

It would have been well boring for me. I went to stay at my mums instead.
I had a look at the jobs in the paper this week. It's not worth going to work for the low wages that people are offering.
I don't know why my dad still works as a doorman, it must be dangerous. He said if I ever considered doing a rubbish job like that, he would be the first person I would have to fight.
He wants me to go to college, university etc but that won't give me all the things I want. These trainers cost me £120 and this Jacket £100. I'm glad I don't get in fights like my dad did when he was young. No fight is worth ruining my clothes.'

Now compare the two experiences. At 15, I had spent a couple of years in Judo and was now beginning to learn Karate. By this time I had been involved in some kind of confrontation almost every single day that I was at school.

The bullying that I didn't get from school at weekends was made up for from the bullying that I received from my father at home.

Call them fights, beatings, confrontations, discipline, education or anything you want, the fact is that by the time I was taking my first ever belt in Karate. I had encountered literally hundreds of fights. I was adding Martial arts to how I already felt about life and the people around me.

I could spot a bully a mile off and within Karate, I found just as many bullies existed as they did in my personal life.

My son's life took a somewhat different route. I fought bitterly for custody of him for seven year until I finally won. From the age of seven to 15, I took care of his every want and need as far as I possibly could.

He was sheltered from the seedier rougher side of life - although we still lived in the rough neighbourhoods of Tottenham, Canning Town, and Basildon.

I trained him in the martial arts and he was at brown belt level by 15 years old when he gave up training. He was not a fighter. I suppose he must have had around four boyish fights in all this time, but nothing that was a real threat.

At 15 he gave up the martial arts because he lost a fight. *'Karate didn't work for me'* was his excuse.

Although I admit that I had never taught him the uglier side of combat. Reason being that this is not the type of stuff I want in the hands of any child, especially my own. His karate techniques would have worked, if he wanted them to.

He was and is still missing that one vital ingredient. The kind of affective learning that people like myself have had in the learning environments that we experienced them in.

My son lives a comfortable life that is a million miles removed from the discomfort that I experienced.

I tried my hardest to find an even balance so that he would have a great childhood that he would remember with fondness, unlike how I view my childhood.

However in doing this, he had to miss out on something.

That being the experiences of the rougher side of life.

I cannot give that to him. I did what I believe most good parents would do. Give their child everything that they never had and make sure that they do not suffer any of the pain that they did as kids. However without pain and discomfort in our lives, their will be some things that we can never truly have and can never truly feel.

I would not change anything about the way I brought him up just to make him 'Tougher.' If he never gets in another fight throughout the rest of his life, I will be happy. Same goes for my other children. Also if he ever attempted to teach self-protection from the angle of having 'Walked the walk', I would be the first to advise him that he needs a career change. There are enough pretenders already out their taking money under false pretences.

Please don't misunderstand me as knocking my children for not being tough. That's not the case at all. I love them dearly and do not want them to be lured into a false sense of security that could get then seriously hurt.

Too many martial arts instructors sadly take their children down the path of giving them a false sense of security.

My son will hate the fact that I have used him as an example, but the truth is, he is not alone, and hopeful this book will help him to also understand that both our lives were vastly different. He cannot be me and I cannot be him.

Too many parents look down on their kids because they do not reach the parents expectations.

Another point that comes to light here is reputations. How many times have we heard it said *'Don't mess with him, he's from the? family they're tough.'*

Its not always the case, but borrowing strength can build weakness.

Many youngsters grow up on the reputation of their father's abilities, or elder brother's etc. Yet they have not had the same experiences as their father or elder brother. So the end result, once again is something quite different.

In fact most would have had even less fights than the average kid because the family name and reputation would keep confrontations at bay.

To further explore my theory on affective learning I have interviewed many people, putting this theory to them. Some questions have been loaded, some are hard, others dig deep into the individuals psychological profile and at least one person interviewed, would not let me dig deep at all, giving brief short answers.

In the interviews that I've conducted. Answers and differences of opinion have gone in all directions.

Some feel that you can teach someone to be tough, others say you can't, and there is also the opinion that there are degrees or levels of toughness that one can achieve, or reach.

I hope that you can take on board the broad range of answers and decide for yourself what you really feel makes tough guys tough.
If you are learning any form of combat art, be it Boxing, Karate, Kung fu, etc for the sole aim to become tough, or tougher than you are now. This book will definitely give you something to think about.

To help you recognise and understand the learning domains, I have included some basic examples that I have extracted from one of my courses.
If you have no interest in the three main ways in which we learn, you can skip the next section. However if you want to understand more about the way in which you personally are being taught, check it out to see if you are missing out on something.
Please ignore the fact that the examples are self defence related, The teaching and learning domain apply to all areas from martial arts to underwater basket weaving.

Teaching via the three domains

If you are not involved in teaching or have no interest in recognising the three learning domains within your training – skip this chapter because you will find it a tad boring.

If the three learning domains are of interest to you and your role as a teacher, look out for my teaching related books later in the year.
If you are a student of a fighting system, I suggest that you read and absorb this section of the book because it will give you an idea as to the type of tuition that you are receiving. It will also highlight any areas or learning domains that you are missing out on.

I will now move on to the classroom or gymnasium scenario to explain the principles of learning further. I will tie these in with some learning objectives ensuring that the different methods of learning are both recognised and used.

This is taken from one of the Self-protection courses that I held.

For this example I have used 5 Learning Objectives linked into my chosen method of learning.

Psychomotor teaching

1. *The Student will be able to gain release from an attacker's Stranglehold* (Psychomotor).

The student learnt how to gain release from a stranglehold. The learning took place due to repetition of the same body mechanics that are required to perform the task. The student will gradually be able to perform the technique in a more natural flowing manner.
The muscle and body movement patterns are psychomotor skills and need to be repeated over a period of time, for the movement to become more natural & flowing.

Cognitive teaching

2. *The student will be able to react, turn and look into the direction that is called out by the tutor I.e. North, South, East, West* (Cognitive).

The students were building up reaction time by being able to turn to the direction called out. The student will have to rely on their ears receiving the command, which is sent to the brain and decoded.

The brain will then send the relevant messages to the body to tell it how to respond to the command. This thinking process is Cognitive because the brain is being used to think and make a decision as to which direction to turn.

Affective teaching

3. *Students will have to explain how they felt when an attacker grabbed them in an aggressive manner* (Affective).

The student will experience the feeling of being grabbed and being at risk. They will feel a rush of Adrenaline, short breaths, and sweaty palms. This area of learning is to have the experience of how it feels to be confronted. This area of learning is Affective because it includes their feelings, attitudes, emotions, and values.

Psychomotor teaching

4. *Students will be able to demonstrate a hand strike on the heavy bag* (Psychomotor).

In this lesson the student had to learn the skills of correctly closing the hand to make a fist. Then the hand, Arm, Shoulder, & Waist must move in a set manner to enable the bone and muscle groups to work together to perform the technique.

Co-ordination is a big part of this lesson and all Psychomotor based training sessions. Students learn by repeating the same body movements over and over again.

Psychomotor & Cognitive teaching

5. *Students will be able to react to their partners Foot or Hand strikes with a deflection* **(Psychomotor & Cognitive).**

The students are first presented with a thinking and decision process. This involves the Brains thought mode, which is cognitive. The student will then have to decide within seconds whether they are going to defend against a lower body foot attack or higher body hand attack.

This decision process involves the brain so is cognitive. The student then has to use their psychomotor skills to perform the correct body movements to enable them to deflect the oncoming attack.

Overview

Some students find the psychomotor skills easier to learn whereas others are able to react much faster using the cognitive process of learning. The younger group aged around the mid 20s were generally much more capable of learning via all three domains of Psychomotor, Cognitive, and Affective forms of learning.

The 40-year-olds and upward seemed to have a much harder task of learning the Psychomotor and Cognitive way but the Affective way appeared the same for everybody.
I found that I had to break down the psychomotor skills into their smallest possible units in order for the older members of the group and those that had a slower learning ability.

The Affective side of learning began to lose its effect after a few repetitions of the same type of attack because the fear factor had gone and the element of safety became accepted.
I learnt that the Affective form of learning will have to be kept to a level where the students still feel the elements involved in

being attacked and that when this feeling begins to disappear, maybe after a few repetitions, I must then change to another type of threat that will get the students Adrenaline pumping.

In the future, Students can develop their own powers of learning by doing some of the following things.

Psychomotor:

The student can form a physical exercise routine that closely resembles the psychomotor skill that they are trying to achieve.

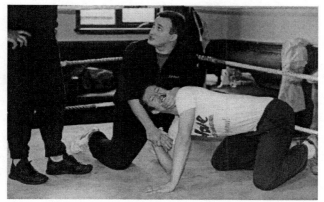

Teaching psychomotor skills to Terry Marsh & Glen Murphy

E.g. A simple Press-up/Push-up exercise will give you the same psychomotor skill, body movement, & co-ordination that you would need to push somebody away who becomes to close to you. This exercise resembles the true self-defence technique as closely as possible. It may even represent the need to support yourself if one of your points of balance are taken away.

Affective:

*The nearest I will ever get to being
in the ring with a World Champion*

This part of the training can be practised in our daily Life by doing anything that will set off the flow of adrenaline. Facing our own fears or phobias will do this.

E.g. If we are petrified of spiders, we can go and visit the local pet store and get as close as we can to the spider.

If we are frightened to get in the boxing ring, we can work in a boxer's corner for a while. This would take us a minute step closer towards the feeling of actually being in there. Not quite that same panicky feeling that we would get in a real-life attack but still a step forward.

Cognitive:

This process of learning can be used daily, even whilst laying in bed relaxing because it only involves the brain.

We can repeatedly go over the same movement in our head just like we are rewinding a videotape and think about the different ways that we could react to various threat situations.
It's a bit like having a controlled daydream, but you are in control of your thought movements.

So what's next?

If you want to be hard, tough, or whatever you want to call it, you will have to go through the experiences that affect your feelings-attitude-emotions & values.
One way or the other -you will have to walk the walk!

The problem here is that, as adults, we are very much set in our ways and conditioned to a certain way of thinking. It is hard to teach an old dog new tricks, but even harder to teach someone how to feel. If at all!

If you were to put a naked flame to my skin and try to train me to be happy- you are going to get nowhere. What I feel is what I feel! No matter what you tell me.

To apply this to 'feeling or becoming hard' creates the same problem. If I teach you psychomotor skills which will enable you to knock a man out with one punch, and teach you the theory of confrontation and what approach to use-giving you the cognitive skills, you will still be short of the most important ingredient, **Affective learning**.

I can tell you not to feel scared, not to shake, not to get emotional, not to let reputations worry you etc but when it actually kicks off, you will uncontrollably feel - what you feel.

Your Psychomotor and Cognitive skills will not be any different, everything that I have taught you will be the same, but the **hidden area of learning-affective learning**, will be the real deciding factor in the outcome of the confrontation.

I know people that can think what to do when it kicks off, have the motor fitness skills to back it up, but are missing the vital ingredient, the conditioning of affective learning.

The learning environment

The learning environment is such an important factor to our affective learning. I cannot begin to count the number of times I have come across martial art black belts who are preaching the philosophies of the street survivalist without ever having had the experiences.

I often ask them about the learning environment from which they are drawing this vast amount of fighting & survival knowledge from and receive some very colourful answers, but rarely the truth.

Granted, there are many people out there that have as many or more street life experiences than me, but for every martial arts black belt out there to have experienced the reality of the street? I don't think so.

In fact not many have. A majority of martial arts instructors are only speculating about what they would do in a real fight, and in turn, they listen to their own stories so much that they begin to convince themselves that they actually had this exiting past.

They go on to teach their philosophies based on this, to people that do not know any different. These students then go on to become instructors themselves and the lie goes on.

The blind leading the blind.

A guy that my father shared his cell with in prison was an expert on cars and car repairs. Anything you wanted to know about any car, he knew it. Yet he had never worked on a car in his life and didn't even know how to drive.

However he had a fascination for cars and had plenty of time on his hands in which to read everything available on the subject that he could get access to.

Some people do a similar thing with pop stars that become a fascination for them. In some instances, the fans can quote more facts about someone than that person can even remember themselves..

Many martial arts instructors do the same thing. There fascination for the arts takes then along a journey of collecting and storing information about the subject.

The missing and all-important attribute is the learning environment where affective learning takes its toll on your feelings, attitude, emotions and values.

They are like the car expert who has never driven or worked on a car, or the obsessed fan that does not have day-to-day contact with the pop star yet knows everything about them.

Nothing can replace affective learning in the real environment. The nearest we can get to it is simulation. But how comfortable would you really feel as a passenger of a plane piloted by someone that has <u>only</u> ever had experience of a flight simulator. In many ways it could be compared to a **Fight** Simulator. Practising fighting that is not for real!

In any self protection class it is possible to introduce a few lessons that touch on the affective domain so you can experience Fear, hate, winning, losing, crying, and all the other emotions that you get from life. But to be honest, you will not even scratch the surface of having a short section of true-life real experiences.

Also there is only a small amount of mileage that you can get from affective learning in any class or course before you eventually become desensitised to it.

Take a look at the classes, which are taken by male instructor's teaching females anti rape techniques.

How can any male begin to conceive the feeling of any female truly fearing rape?

I teach female self-protection as one of my main fields, but I could never explain the <u>feeling</u> of fearing rape.

It's not a concept that even enters the male mind unless we were going to be institutionalised or imprisoned. We do not, and have not experienced the **feelings** **attitude** **emotions** and **values** that a female would attach to such an emotion subject.

I don't know any male that fears being raped by a member of the opposite sex. I cannot conceive what that would feel like.

In short, we do not have the same affective learning as females do in this area. This is why the average kick punch martial arts course for women is a total waste of time. You have dry land swimmers once again teaching in ignorance.

Even if it is a female instructor who can express how this kind of fear feels – they are still normally lacking other types of exposure to affective learning due to their learning environment.

I have included a chapter called '**The evolution of female self protection**' to try and highlight even further the difference between men and women in regards to toughness, affective learning, and the learning environment, and values.

Me cross training in 1982 along with many others

Feeling how it is?

To teach via affective learning, you will have to give the student exposure and understanding of people in particular situations. To do this you will have to create an activity that the student is unfamiliar with, so that they cam feel what its like to be in someone else's shoes. You will be simulating a situation by creating an affective learning role-play activity.

For example they could play the part of a doorman and have other members within the group playing the part of awkward customers, even confronting and challenging them. This way they will be a step nearer to feeling the situation opposed to seeing the situation.
The same could be done to give students the feeling of being bullied, being a decision-maker, being a teacher, being a minority, enforcing justice etc.

In my self-protection classes, I make each student take a micro lesson as the tutor so that they can actually feel what it's like to pass on knowledge. Maybe this sounds easy, but to do this for a class of experienced people who are encouraged to give feedback at the end of the lesson is something else. I also video the session so the student can watch themselves on TV and see what others see. The affective learning though is actually being out there in front of the class with groups of focussed eyes watching your every move. It is felt and cannot be gained by any other method.

Can you imagine how it feels to be asked, *'how do you know that technique actually works?'* It makes you think about every little thing that you do and say, and hopefully the students become good instructors. There is a difference between being a shit instructor and a shit hot instructor.

Anybody can pass on a technique to a friend or neighbour in the back garden, but if you want to be a good experienced teacher, you will have to do it within the necessary learning environment that touches on your feelings, attitude and emotions.

Another example:

We all know what an elderly person represents to us 'generally.' But how many of us actually know what it feels like to be elderly? None of us. It's an affective experience that they have had which we still have to come (depending on your current age).   If you wanted to get a step closer to how if feels to be elderly you are going to have to simulate them as closely as possible. So what would you do from you current level of understanding? Arch your back, squint your eyes, pretend not to hear, move about slowly... This will not give you affective learning because you can switch any of these choices off as and when they become uncomfortable.

Try this method of affective learning:
Put a couple of dried peas in each shoe so that you will be forced to walk in a fashion to avoid discomfort. Put on a pair of spectacles but smear the lens with Vaseline so the eyes see the world with impaired vision. Put some cotton wool in your ears to restrict your hearing. Put on rubber gloves to restrict hand movement and sense of touch. Then spend a few hours on everyday things tasks like using the tv, telephone, newspaper, putting the rubbish out, making a meal, and if brave enough-a walk to the shops. This is true affective learning.
I always choose a type of person or situation that I want my students to learn about. But also remind them that this is only an insight to how it feels and nothing can replace true-life experiences in the necessary learning environments.

Have a think about the above examples and see how affective learning is helping us to become whatever we are. Tougher, just being one of those things.

The interviews

As part of my research into what makes tough guys tough, I decided to interview people that were involved in a variety of fields but who have all had involvement with people connected to violence of some shape or form.

They are all professionals within their field, be it Martial artist, Soldier of fortune, Boxer, Street fighter, Bodyguard etc.

You will know some names whereas others will not be names that you would have come across before. However, I must say that every interview I have done is of equal importance so urge you to read all of them rather than just the names that are familiar to you.

The most interesting thing about each of the interviews is that I have kept the questions pretty much the same and none of the people interviewed were aware of the answers given by any of the others. So all answers and opinions will be fresh and without cohesion.

You are now being given the opportunity to find out what these individuals really think about 'what makes tough guys tough.' Unfortunately, at the time of writing, I was unable to find any females that were prepared to take part in the interview process.

Geoff Thompson
Author of
Many books related to Self-protection.
Co-Chief Instructor of the British Combat Association

Jamie: Geoff, if I was to ask you what you feel makes tough guys tough, what would your answer be?

Geoff T: *Being tough is an entirely cerebral concept.*
It is not about being physically tough, though physical adversity, hard training etc, is one way of developing toughness.

In my lifetime I have met very few people who are 'tough' in the true sense of the word. I've met many that are tough within their own arena and yet relatively soft outside of it.

The few that I have met who are truly tough have always been the most unlikely, as in they do not wear their toughness like a badge for all to see, if they did then I'd say that they were insecure as opposed to tough.

Jamie: Can you define at least one attribute that you would attach to a tough guy?

Geoff T: *Generally the 'made it' guy would be of polarised character who, metaphorically speaking; keeps his toughness hidden under his jacket like a magnum, only to be drawn when necessity calls. 95% of the time a real tough guy will appear to the majority to be a normal, even soft, person. When he switches on it will appear almost like a metamorphosis.*

Jamie: I believe that anyone can go to a class and learn the Physical -psychomotor side of an art and the Cognitive problem solving side, like "what to do if X happens. But I do not feel that you can learn the feelings - attitude - emotions - and values of Affective learning, which I believe can only come from life's experiences, making you what you are, be it tough or soft, bully or victim, etc. What are your views on this?

Geoff T: *Many people have said to me that you can teach a man the physical aspects of fighting but if he hasn't got 'bottle' he'll never have bottle! And you can't teach him that.*
*If I thought for a single second that this was true I'd never take another penny for teaching martial arts. You **can** give them bottle with the right kind of teaching.*

Jamie: Have you managed to accomplish this?

Geoff T: *Yes! I have proven this many times over with my own students. What I will say however is that, they have to want it like they have never wanted anything in their life, because the price that they will be forced to pay on the journey is a very high one. And so it should be.*

Jamie: Why should it be?

Geoff T: *The acquisition of courage where there was none before changes lives for the better and forever. I would also agree, of course that there is no real substitute for encountering the 'real' thing.*

Jamie: But there is no such thing as the real thing in the fighting arts is there? Real is real and anything less than that cannot be real, can it? I personally think that we all make our own choice as to how near we are prepared to go within our training to get as close as possible to the real world. Some get pretty close whereas other are as far as they possibly can get from reality. Where does your teaching fit into the scheme of things?

Geoff T: *What I do via my 'Animal Day' type training is give the practitioners the first few levels of courage needed to confront their own fears and therefore gain greater life experiences. This then will take them to higher levels of courage and therefore higher levels of consciousness. We must never forget either that extremely hard, confrontational training is in itself a 'life experience.'*

Jamie: So if I was the most passive person on this planet - afraid of my own shadow, could I be converted into a tough guy, afraid of no one?

Geoff T: *Yes, certainly you could for all of the forementioned reasons, but it would have to be your life's quest, to the detriment of all other things, to do so.*
And the work would have to be done by you and no one else. A good teacher would serve as a guide for this type of person. He would give them the map and the fuel, but they've still got to drive the car themselves.

I have to clarify one point though, a person should not expect to become 'afraid of no one on the planet', fear, as long as you understand the mechanics of it, is a healthy thing. It is good to feel fear as long as you know when and how to override it if a situation needs fronting.
Some situations should not be met, and flight is the right and healthy choice.

Jamie: So how are we to know when to choose 'fight or flight?'

51

Geoff T: *It takes wisdom to know when to run and when to stand and fight, this is a by-product of the training needed to acquire this so-called fearlessness. So there is no such thing as fearing no man, you will and should always feel fear, it is survival's early warning system to protect the species from extinction. Your goal should be to completely understand the physiological aspects of fear and to develop a strong enough will to over ride the natural instinct to run should a situation need fronting.*

But to answer your question, yes, with the right information, the right map and the right guide you can go anywhere, be anything. I believe this with all of my heart.

Also, I quite often find that under matured people, those that can have a bit of a fight and who have seen a bit of life, sometimes become pretentious, feeling that, because they have perhaps faced a few situations down and exercised their bottle successfully, they are a little special and that they are gifted with courage and the others who haven't got it will never get it.

I don't believe this to be the case. Anyone can open the lock if they have the right combination.

Jamie: Some people seem to feel that becoming a black belt is the answer to being tough, Does a Martial art Black belt mean someone is tough, if not - what does it mean?

Geoff T: *Having a black belt in a martial can mean a lot and it can mean nothing at all, depending upon where and how you achieved the grade.*

It is not the belt its self that means anything, though the goal of achieving it is necessary on the journey, it is the journey you take that is important. The end is important in the journey but it is the journey that is important in the end.

Jamie: So what does the black belt mean to you?

Geoff T: *To me a black belt is like a university degree, once achieved you go out into the world and do something with it.*

If you don't leave university and get some real experience then it is worth little more than the paper that it is written on. Black belt is a fundamental, predominantly physical level.

The higher Dan's should be relative to your physical, mental and spiritual development. If for instance you are a 3rd Dan martial artist and still struggling with fundamental disciplines like personal hygiene, regular training routine, diet, good manners etc then I don't believe that they are quite up to that grade.

This doesn't mean that you can't have a fight, many people with poor willpower can still go toe to toe for five minutes but at third Dan it is the intangible qualities that I would be looking at.

At 4th Dan one should be working at and mastering negative emotions like greed, envy, spite, maliciousness, jealousy, uncontrolled anger etc etc. The higher the grade the more control you should be able to exercise over the self.

Above 4th Dan I believe that it becomes more spiritual and self-mastery comes into its own. This is where you nurture a profound understanding of the self and others, this allows you to forgive yourself and forgive others.

It allows you to see that we share the same universe and that there is room for everyone. At this level you will be nurturing pure love, even for those that have no love for you, even those that hate you. And I don't mean this in a patronising way, 'look at me I'm forgiving my enemies.'

I mean it truly in a sense that forgiveness is a great strength, a great exercise of spiritual will and a great way to stop the hate of grudge that corrodes you from the inside out.

If a guy is carrying a 5th Dan, or a 6th Dan or a 7th Dan and he is still frightened of sharing, he's jealous, he deceives his wife, he lies, robs, sells drugs, steals, loathes, hates, intimidates, threatens etc etc etc then he has reached an embryonic peak, he's still a nine stone weakling on the inside.

I know people of this grade and above that are still on the physical plane, some of them are little more than playground bullies.

It's sad, I feel a lot of compassion for these people because their life is full of pain, they see everything as a threat. I know of one or two that send out anonymous hate mail to rivals. I mean you tell me, is that action of a master grade or an insecure green belt?

Jamie: So if being a black belt does not mean your tough! Can you put all the tough guys you know of, into any sort of category? I.e. they are mostly from the forces, or mostly from broken homes etc.

Geoff T: *Yes! I could place them all into one category. They have all exercised their will and fought against the natural instinct to be comfortable.*
That's the key, to find the sauce you must swim against the stream. When you do this you will be one of the very few, which can be very lonely at times.

When you are on the wrong path you will know also because there will be crowds and crowds swimming with you. If your journey is uncomfortable then it is usually the right path.
The background of such leaders is usually incidental to their achievements, it is what they do as opposed to where they come from that determines where they are going.

Like the old saying 'it is attitude and not aptitude that determines altitude'.

What I will say is that quite often the background of a person, a broken home, time in the forces etc can act as a catalyst for success but only if they exercise their will to make it so.
Jamie: Can you take somebody and make him or her tough? If not what is the nearest you can get them, to what you consider as being tough?

Geoff T: *You can temper anyone into anything if they can stand the heat of the forge. How far they go along the path is largely determined by how much pain they are willing to incur. It works on the universal law of cause and effect, you reap as you sow. You will get out exactly what you put in. It's that simple.*

Jamie: As a young lad I had a pal, who many others and I considered to be the toughest person we had ever known. He was a brilliant street fighter who was rarely defeated. I met him 15 years later and he was a shadow of him former self, practically flinching if anyone came near him in a threatening manner. It was like his spirit had been broken. Do you think a tough guy can be made to be or become un-tough?

Geoff T: *Yes, for sure I have always found that if you don't use it you will lose it'. If you don't exercise muscle it will atrophy. The same goes for anything else. If you leave a car in the garage for a year and then take it out for a spin the chances are it will have seized up from under use. You have to exercise everything if you want to keep it keen.*
Once you have developed mental toughness it is important that you exercise it via your will. By making your self do the things in life that are uncomfortable, by getting to the dojo when you are feeling lazy, by attacking and having daily battles with your own weakness, by stepping into adversity. You can maintain your wares forever if you keep the blade to the grindstone. If you don't you should expect it to become blunt over time.

Jamie: Do you think it is possible to sense that someone is tough just from the way they carry themselves?

Geoff T: *If you are very perceptive you will see toughness shining from a person like a neon light. It will be so obvious to the enlightened that it will be as if it were tattooed on their forehead. This kind of perception, enlightenment, sixth sense what ever you wish to call it can be developed through good* *martial arts training. Strong people have an aura that is almost tangible. When they walk into a room you know that they are someone. People are drawn to them, animals and children sense it also and are quite often awed by them. This strength is usually cloaked by a kindness and openness that is often mistaken, by the uninitiated, for softness or weakness.*

I say beware the quiet man. The loud, the garrulous, the bullying are generally insecure.

They are posture's not fighters. If I pointed out to you the ten toughest people I know, on face value you would find it hard to believe, they would not fall into type and you'd find yourself saying, 'No! Really?' That's the kind of tough guy that I admire and adhere to.

Teaching with Rick, Paul and Geoff – Coventry 1994

Rick Young from Edinburgh is a good example of this. He is hugely respectful and very humble, yet as an 'out an out' fighter I'd put him in with anyone that I have met on the world stage.

I admire people like Rick because they are not afraid to be emotional, soft, kind, loving. They are not afraid to forgive. Why should they be, they has nothing to prove.

The toughest people I have met on this planet we call earth have all been this way and yes you could sense it when you were near them, it is very awe inspiring.

The 'pretenders' are so obvious that they don't need to be pointed out, they highlight their dearth in the way they carry themselves, in the way they treat those that are of no profit to them, those they feel are a competition to them, every time they open their mouths to speak they bay their lack.

Jamie: Geoff, your respect for Rick Young comes across quite clearly. I have had the privilege of teaching alongside you and Rick on a British Combat course in Coventry and I certainly agree that he is a lovely guy who really knows his stuff. If anyone wants to learn Jeet Kune do, Rick's your man.

Geoff T: *Absolutely, he is a great ambassador for the martial arts and a fine example of the quiet guy who carries his magnum hidden away, and does not go through life acting tough.*

Jamie: Is it possible to act tough without really being tough?

Geoff T: *Yes, definitely. Probably 95% of those that claim to be tough- I don't by the way- are not. The very act of claiming you are usually disqualifies you from being so. If you were hugely confident in your abilities you wouldn't be wearing it in your walk.*

Jamie: How would you deal with a tough guy who is in your face prompting you to kick off with him?

Geoff T: *This is a question that is hard to answer because every situation is different and demands a different solution. But as a general rule of thumb,*
If I had no other option open to me I'd hit him, pre-emptively with everything I had. If I sensed that he was a pretender then I might posture and try to bottle him out.

Jamie: Do you feel that there is a difference between men and women with regards to their toughness. I.e. would you be happy to let women take the place of men on the front line of pubs & clubs etc.?

Geoff T: *Because toughness is a cerebral concept I'd say that men and women could share the same platform as regards toughness, and in this society they quite often do.*

*I would add though that for many women-depending upon how they are brought up, their genes etc, combat toughness would **not** be as easy to attain as it would be for the men, though, again if they wanted it bad enough they could get it.*

Biologically women are not the same as men, you may have noticed and men have always been, traditionally, the hunter and gatherer of the species, and women, the carer's.

This natural balance is based of the universal law of yin and yang, where the strong and the yielding compliment each other, where they co-exist in harmony. In fact I'd go as far as to say that they cannot properly exist without each other.

Jamie: So would you be happy to let women replace men on the door?

Geoff T: *I'd be very happy for a women to share a night club door with me, but not to replace me or other male doormen, rather to work in harmony with us and us with them. There is room for both on the same platform as equals.*

Because society is changing at a race like speed, and because this natural combination has been abused by many males who have down trodden the rights of women, the ladies are rebelling, they are no longer happy with being the carer and long for the excitement of the hunter gatherer, so are shedding the pinny and putting on the overalls (or the dicky bow).

Women are starting to lead in many areas of society, proving to be, just as tough as the men, only without the engorged ego of many male leaders. If they can do this and still retain their femininity I think it is a very good thing.

Jamie: I certainly agree that women do not subscribe to the ego trip as men do. In fact I have tried to get this point across in this book within the section 'The Evolution of female self protection.' The martial arts have certainly played a big part in restricting the female development towards being tougher. What do you feel the role of Martial arts has in making tough guys tough?

Geoff T: *Handling physical adversity, i.e. through training in the martial arts, is the greatest exercise, and builder of the will known to man. A strong will enables you to be in charge of you, and if you are in charge, you have the power, then you can choose to be tough should a situation demand toughness. That's how I feel about myself.*

Jamie: In an earlier answer you said *'Probably 95% of those that claim to be tough, are not- I don't by the way.'* Just to clarify this point. Do you consider yourself to be tough, or are you tough?

Geoff T: *I am not a tough person, but should I choose to be tough to neutralise a potentially violent situation then I can and I will. Once sorted I will switch the toughness off again and become a loving father, doting husband, caring son etc etc. But getting back to your main question of 'what the role of Martial arts play in making tough guys tough?' I would like to add that training in the martial arts took me half way to this realisation and working the doors finished my apprenticeship. However, if there is no real discomfort in your training, if you do not feel fear on the way to the dojo then your chosen martial art becomes a recreational past time that is no more likely to help you develop toughness than stamp collecting.*
The discovery is in the discomfort, hardiness comes through handling discomfort. It has been medically proven that controlled exposure to adrenaline, brought on by confrontational training or whatever, with respite, develops a desensitisation to the discomfort of the syndrome. This could be classed as one example of toughness.

Jamie: Geoff, thank you very much for your time and thoughts on 'what makes tough guys tough.' I know many people will be very interested to read your views on this topic.

Geoff T: *Jamie, thank you for putting your questions to me. This is an excellent idea for a book, which I hope does well for you.*

Jamie: Thank you!

Jamie interviews Geoff

Jamie interviews
Dave 'Boy' Green

Dave 'Boy' Green
Former British and European Welterweight Boxing Champion

Jamie: Dave, we have known each other for over 15 years now. We also worked for a year together on a project, giving us plenty of time to get to know each other.

At the time, we were both proficient in our own fighting arts. Yours being Boxing and myself with martial arts yet even then when things became a little strained or we clashed on things. Neither of us ever resorted to physical solutions or attempted to use our art to resolve things.

For me personally, I was in awe of you and your achievements in boxing and had bundles of respect for you but I don't think you ever recognised it as such.

From my perspective, you were bit of a tough guy who had a heart of gold. I truly admired you.

Many people took to you as their boxing hero and would certainly regard you a tough guy, what are your thoughts on that?

Dave G: *Well as you say, at the time, you knew more of me due to the TV coverage that I did of you as a martial artist but the word that really comes to mind is respect! And that's what it's all really about. You knew that I worked very, very, hard to get where I got and the word respect is what it's all really about.*

Jamie: Do you feel that some people are naturally more respectful that others though, because there are a lot of disrespectful people around.

Dave G: *Oh Yeah! There is definitely. But I think that people respect you for different things. If you're in a Pop group and have a hit, some people respect you for that, if you are a boxer and make it to the top, some people respect you for that. If you're a politician some people respect you for that. Its all down to the effort you put into something that make people respect you for that particular thing.*

Jamie: Do you think that discussing a problem is much better than resorting to violence?

Because you fought Sugar Ray Leonard and many other boxers, over 105 amateur and 41 professional fights, so being physical and using your fists to solve a problem would have come easy.

Dave G: *Yeah but that's not the answer, it never finishes there does it! It just goes further and further and adds more people into the world of violence, including your family etc.*

Jamie: So you much prefer the discussion approach to the fighting approach!

Dave in training with Joe Bugner

Dave G: *Absolutely! Everytime.*

Jamie: If I were to ask you what you feel makes tough guys tough, what would your answer be?

Dave G: *Well to me, I think you're born with it. Its a mental attitude, its determination, you're either tough or you're not tough.*
I do think it helps as well coming from a rough background, although I'm an exception to the rule. I did not live in a rough area, my parents always loved me but you find that a lot of rough fellows come from rough upbringing.

Jamie: But that wasn't the case for you?

Dave G: *Not at all. My father had a farm, he was a farmer. I think I just had the determination to get to the top.*

Jamie: Do you think you would have succeeded in anything that you went into?

Dave G: *Well my manager Andy Smith said to me that I should go into business when I finished boxing and he was right. I've proved again that I can be successful. I have a Company & factory that has been distributing to all the major banks since I left the ring, I have 6 houses, timeshares in Florida, a couple of Cash Converter stores, Stocks and shares and so on. I'm not saying this to be flash. I'm just trying to make the point that it was in me to succeed in whatever I went into.*

Jamie: Your success in not that common for retired boxers is it?

Dave G : *Definitely not,*
in fact it's not that common for Sports people in general. When I
turned professional and got
married I had absolutely
nothing! All my money came
afterwards.

I had a very good manager
who looked after me and
made sure I looked after my
money and taught me the
right ways to do it.

I think whatever you do in
life, you need somebody
above you to look after you
and make sure you do the
right things.

I was very lucky in that aspect
because Andy Smith was like
a father figure to me.

He made me realise that boxing only goes on for so long maybe
6, 8 to ten years.

Mine was only seven years but he made me realise that there is
a lot of living to be done afterwards and I'm pleased I took his
advice.

Jamie: Yeah, I suppose you could have ignored his advice and
stayed in boxing and ended up with nothing.

Dave G: *Absolutely that's why he was such a good manager. I had won two British titles, two European titles, and fought twice for the World championship and I was never going to be in the position to fight for a world title again so I took his advice and got out and did something else while I could.*

Jamie: So to put it into a nutshell, you were born with that ability, and didn't go and actually learn how to be tough.

Dave G: *No I don't think so. I've always had it in me. I used to play a lot of football then progressed to boxing but was always aggressive with everything I went into. I would always put 120% into everything I did, no matter what it was I was doing. It's determination.*

Jamie: I believe that anyone can go to a class and learn the Physical psychomotor skills, the physical movements. Like taking a young lad through the movements of Boxing, Karate etc.
Also I believe you can teach then how to think for example if a certain type of punch is thrown to bob, weave, duck, whatever.

You can teach them to do certain combination of punches which draws on the cognitive thinking side like, but I do not feel that you can learn the feelings - attitude - emotions - and values that you get from Affective learning, which I believe can only come from your upbringing & life's experiences, making you what you are, be it tough or soft, bully or victim, etc. What is your view on this?

Dave G: *I think you're born with it. You're either an aggressive person, or have the will to win, toughness, call it what you want. You just can't put that into someone, you've either got it or you've not got it.*

Jamie: Toughness sounds a silly word but it's convenient to use for the purpose of my research.

Dave G: *Yeah, but I understand what you're trying to say. Toughness comes in many different ways.*

Jamie: Of course, but many people have watched people like yourself, Mo Hussein, Terry Marsh, etc in the ring and want to be like that. They want to know what makes you that tough?

Dave G: *I'm not tough in the world. I'm just as friendly as anybody else in real life. But when I put a pair of gloves on and got in that ring, my personality changed.*

Jamie: That's the same thing Mo Hussein said to me when I approached him for an interview. I'm not tough.

It appears that all the guys that are tough in their own arena are also very modest and humble and try to play down their aggressive tougher side.

If I was the most passive person on this planet - afraid of my own shadow, could I be trained and converted into a tough guy, afraid of no one?

Dave G: *Again I would say no! You're born with it, you just can't teach people to be tough.*

Jamie: You're well known for your Boxing ability and obviously you have had exposure to boxers of all levels. Does a Boxing title mean someone is tough, if not - what does it represent?

Dave G: *It represents many different things to me. It means some people are very skilful, some have got loads of heart, a person like myself has lots of determination but it doesn't mean that they are tough. I've met some great fighters who are very skilful but they are not tough*

Jamie: Could you put all the tough guys you know of, into any sort of category? I.e. they are mostly from the forces, or mostly from broken homes etc.

Dave G: *No not really. Because I come from a good family, I'm not saying that my father had loads of money but he was comfortable. I think generally they come from rough areas like your Liverpool's, Newcastle, the East End and like where things are generally tougher. But there are always odd people like myself who are successful or tough in other areas.*

Jamie: If as you say, you cannot make somebody tough, is it all to do with how you're brought up. What is the nearest you can get them, to what you consider as being tough?

Dave G: *You can't make anybody tough, you have either got it or you haven't. That's my own personal opinion on it.*

Jamie: As a young lad I had a pal, who was a tough and brilliant street fighter who was rarely defeated. I met him 15 years later and he was a shadow of his former self, practically flinching if anyone came near him in a threatening manner. It was like his spirit had been broken. Do you think a tough guy can be made to be or become un-tough?

Dave G: *No I just think its approach and a different attitude to life. He was a tough little guy who doesn't think it means anything to be tough now.*

Jamie: What like he has matured.

Dave G: *That it, he's matured. When he was growing up he probably thought he had to be tough to be noticed but now its no longer important to him. Your not going to believe this but when I was at junior school, the best fighter in our year was a girl, it certainly wasn't me. She was the toughest one in our year.*

Jamie: . Do you think it is possible to sense that someone is tough just from the way they carry themselves?

Dave G: *No not really, I think people do try and act tough but you just cant tell. I've seen ordinary fellows who are bloody hard as nails. You just can't tell.*

Jamie: You don't think you can just sense it when someone walks into a room?

Dave G: *No! Because I've seen some great boxers who have won championships who don't even look tough at all.*

Jamie: Is it possible to act tough without really being tough?

Dave G: *Yeah! Anybody can act tough can't they, it's easy to act tough, but it's about being able to handle yourself at the end of the day.*

Jamie: Most of us have had to do it sometime in our life right back to schooldays to stop ourselves getting beaten up.

Dave G: *That's right, and we don't want to take that chance of fighting incase we lose so we act tough, hoping that this will win the fight without fighting.*

Jamie: I think this is a major time in our lives no matter what age we are, that we must cross the barrier of acting tough to actually having that fight and taking our first step towards being tough.

Dave: *Absolutely, but even if you have that first fight be it in the ring, or the street, Its the one that has toughness inbred within*

them that will go on to be tough whether they win the first fight or not.

Jamie: How would you deal with a tough guy who is in your face prompting you to kick off with him? Have you ever had that situation?

Dave G: *I've had it a couple of times even when I had my title in boxing. My message to everybody is run like hell, get out the way.*
As I've always said, if you're in a pub and someone wants to fight you, there's no promoter there to give you money afterwards.

You could end up getting a good hiding for nothing. So you might as well just get away. There are plenty more pubs to drink in.

Jamie: We touched on this next question earlier regarding the girl in your junior school. With regards to the toughness of male and female. Would you be happy to let women take the place of men on the front line of pubs & clubs etc.?

Dave G: *I don't think so. I believe its men for some jobs and ladies for other jobs. You can't do that.*

Jamie: Some would regard that as bit of a sexist viewpoint.

Dave G: *No, no.. I mean, like boxing, I've seen the ladies boxing in Las Vegas. It's terrible, horrible. You see a lovely pretty girl with a bleeding nose, to me its just unbelievable, I don't believe in it at all. What do you think?*

Jamie: Well morally, I would not feel comfortable sitting in a factory packing bullets while the women were out there fighting in the front line.

Dave G: *How can anyone sit indoors looking after the kids while the wife is out earning the living as a professional boxer. It just doesn't sound right does it? Mind you, we could be better looking then, ha!*

Jamie: I don't think that would help us though, I think were beyond saving.

Dave G: *I don't think many women would want to carry our broken noses around. Also even in your days as a doorman. It was naturally a male dominated profession and it just wouldn't look right having a woman on the door.*

Jamie: Why?

Dave G: *Because you want to feel you're secure. You're better off with a six foot four chap standing there and ready to deal with any problems, who can sort it out very quickly.*

Jamie: So are you saying that men only feel secure being looked after by other men who look tough.

Dave G: *Absolutely.*

Jamie: What do you feel the role of Boxing has in making tough guys tough?

Dave G: *Well its very difficult to say, I just think it dedication, ability, training, you've got to believe in yourself. I just can't really pinpoint one thing.*
It's many things but for me, I've got to say, before I fought Carlos Palomino for the world championship which was my 25th fight, having been unbeaten 24 times.
I really believed I was unbeatable. But when you do get beat, it takes something away from you. It's no different to being in the street. It just takes something away from you. Did you ever experience that?

Jamie: Yeah, I must admit. As a young black belt I thought I was unbeatable in the street. Whether through luck or skill I was winning fights with ease, but the biggest awakening I had was when one guy pulverised me.

He didn't give a toss as to what belt I was. He kicked my arse. It was the biggest favour anyone had done for me.

I changed the way in which I train from that day on.

The sad thing though was that up until that day I loved Karate but losing that fight took that away from me. I have never enjoyed the art since. Silly really, because it wasn't Karate that lost the fight, it was me. Same as it was you that was beaten on your 25th fight and not the fault of boxing.

Dave G: *I think it proves to everybody that you never stop learning. That's what it's about.*

Jamie: When you first ever took me to your house, I saw a picture on your living room wall of Sugar Ray Leonard. You had so much respect for him and will never be able to forget your fight with him. Do you regard him as being tough?

Dave G: *I regard him as being a complete boxer really, he could fight, he could box, he could move, he was a very intelligent fellow.*

I think he's perhaps the nearest we have ever been to the most complete fighter in the world. Not because he beat me, everybody thinks I'm biased, but I thought that Muhammad Ali was the greatest fighter ever. But I regarded Ali as lacking one thing, the big punch.

Ali was not a big puncher at all. He beat people by a combination of punches but Sugar Ray could do everything that Ali could do but he could punch as well. That's why I think I have so much respect for him.

I also think it was very nice of him to have respect for myself to come over to England to see me.

I think that's what you get in sportsmanship really, in all sports.

Jamie: But even with all you've said about Sugar Ray Leonard, you still haven't answered my question,

Do you think he is tough?

Dave G: *Oh! I think he's tough, I think he's tough, definitely tough. Even though Duran beat him on points, in the next fight he made Duran look like a bit averse with Duran retiring in round five.*

Jamie: I can also remember a time around 12 years ago, when you were watching videotapes of Sugar Ray, I was watching video of you and your son was watching videotapes of me doing my martial arts.
Do you think that toughness is seem more in the eye of the beholder rather than the holder, meaning that we always regard others as being tough rather than ourselves.?

Dave G: *I still have those tapes, the twins watch them now. Yes I do think toughness is seen more in the eye of the beholder. I often say, 'Christ, he's a bloody tough guy' when talking about someone that is not connected to fighting in any shape or form. Then someone will say to me, 'you've got to be joking, your twice as tough as him', but we don't see it in ourselves do we? We definitely see it more in other people.*

Jamie:. I can remember once sitting in your Mercedes waiting for you when a group of lads came over to get a glimpse of you. Although you weren't there, they spotted your numberplate DAV 8OY, which looked like DAV BOY (Dave Boy).

We began chatting and it took me a while to convince them that I was not a boxer. They decided that I must be an East End gangster purely because of the way I speak and look and that I must be your driver. I mention this because I know many people associate toughness with areas like the East end, Glasgow, and so on and many boxing fans actually thought that you were from the east end, which your not. Do you think that areas or accents have any bearing or connection with being tough?

Dave G: *I've still got the personalised plate but the mercs gone, I've had one or two merc's since then.*

As for accents! I do definitely, if someone comes from Glasgow and you hear that Glaswegian accent, you think Christ, he's from Glasgow. I had the greatest time of my life in Glasgow; I came back in stitches Ha! But seriously, the East end have a reputation for being hard, Glasgow, Liverpool, and you get a lot of good fighters from each of these places.

I am just a one off from the Fens but tough within my art as you are with your martial arts, but you also have the East End accent to go with it.

My accent doesn't conjure up the image of toughness.

So I would say that accents do have a connection with toughness but more so because you are exposed to many people who are tough that have the same regional accents.

I would say toughness is in you, regardless of your accent but some accents make you less likely to becoming a target for a bully. I certainly think that the east end accent is a tough accent.

Jamie: Can you be tough and still be nice?

Dave G: *Look at Brian Jacks!*

I did the TV show Superstars with him about 10 times now an what a lovely guy he is, but boy is he tough but a very nice man. There's different ways of being tough..

When he was 15 his father sent him to Japan to train..He couldn't speak a word of Japanese and that toughened him up as well. What a tough man. He stayed out there for two years to learn the business properly.

In fact I played golf with him last week. I was also chatting to Glen Murphy from London's Burning. He's a mate of yours isn't he?

Jamie: Yeah, I know Glen. His dad ran a pub called the Bridgehouse in Canning Town, East London where we all grew up. Glen went into boxing and I went into martial arts. Later on he came to train with me along with Terry Marsh to gain their black belts in my New Breed training system.

Glen had to give up due to a back injury and Terry could not get leave from Brixton prison to come and train, so both came to a natural end.

Dave thanks for answering my questions. On a final note, will you please give me some of you boxing background, as I know many people will be interested in your achievements.

Dave G: *Sure, but first I want to say thank you for spending time and including me in your book. Your other books are very*

76

good and I really hope that this one does well for you. You deserve it.

Jamie: Thank you.

Dave G: *My pleasure...... O.K. I turned professional in 1974. I had 105 amateur fights, and I lost 104, well you can't win them all can you Ha!*
No .. I won about 82 so I wasn't a great amateur but my style was a professional boxing style and I had 24 fights unbeaten.
In that 24 fights I won the British and European light welterweight championship. And the next fight was for a world welterweight championship, which I lost in 11 rounds to Carlos Palomino.
I was well winning the fight right up to the 10th round when my eye closed up and he knocked me out in the 11th. Full credit to Palomino, it just shows you what world champions are made of.
Then I went on and won the British and European welterweight championship and I was lucky enough from there that my manager Andy Smith got me another fight for the world title against Sugar Ray Leonard. That man was the best man I have ever seen in my life. He knocked me out in the fourth round. I honestly believe that If I would have trained for 25 years I would have never beaten him. Anyway after that fight which was my 36th fight I had five more fights, of which I won four. On losing the last one Andy Smith said its time to get out. He loved me as a person and not just as a vehicle to make money for him and I respected that. He could have kept me going for another two or three years making money but he loved me too much for that. So I won two British, two European, and had two shots at the world title and still come out with nearly all my marbles.

Jamie: How many did you have to start off with? Laughs!....

Dave G: *Not many. (Laughs)*

How much will Cash Converters give me for these books?

David Turton 8th DAN
Chief Instructor Self Defence Federation

Jamie: Dave, if I was to ask you what you feel makes tough guys tough, what would your answer be?

Dave T: *Toughness, guts, bravery etc, is a state of mind. The guy who feels 'tough', is in fact someone with control over their own fears.*

The self-same thing might prevent others from entering situations.

Jamie: Can you give an example that we can relate to?

Dave T: *When there is a challenge, be it physical or mental, the real 'tough' guy is the one who overcomes trepidation and meets it.*

Jamie: I believe that anyone can go to a class and learn the Physical psychomotor side of an art and the cognitive problem solving side like 'what to do if X happens.'

But I do not feel that you can learn the feelings - attitude - emotions - and values of Affective learning which I believe only comes from life's experiences. Thus making you what you are, be it tough or soft, bully or victim, etc. What are your views on this?

Dave T: *Jamie, You have in fact just about answered this question yourself, judging by your comments. Being a 'coward' for instance takes on different ideas to different people. It may*

mean to a lot of people, simply someone who is unwilling to enter into fights.
Yet the same person may for example be the bravest Fireman ever, entering into life threatening situations that others may balk at.

Jamie: Can you define a coward?

Dave T: *A coward is really only someone who allows their fears to take control of them, rather than the other way round.*
Bullies, victims, cowards and heroes, are all products of their experiences, and the ways those experiences have been dealt with. It's their affective learning, which you are researching within this book.

Bullies obtain ego gratification through a use of intimidatory methods. The 'Bully' gets a feed back of fear from his/her victims, thus giving him a false belief of being 'hard', and that no-one will stand up to him. Bullies have to target their victims for the bullying to be successful. After all, an unsuccessful bullying session would produce the wrong feed back.

Some people are perennial victims, in that they expect to be a victim, so they play that role. It's a role they are in fact very comfortable with, so they play it. Because they may have successfully deterred violence through compliance, they often use for them, what has been in fact a successful form of defence.
If these people are victims of the 'bully' type, then often the pleading and cowering is enough to gratify the bully, and thus save the coward

But YES, we are ALL products of our experiences. Early experiences forge us in directions that vary, because of the different types of experiences we get.
Familiarisation with violence for example, may make us slightly desensitised to it as you quite rightly highlighted in the last chapter of your book 'Dogs don't know kung fu' under the heading 'Desensitised.' It can also harden us to it. Thus making

it easier to enter into a violent state, that is often in fact the 'normal' response to us.

Pacifism on the other hand especially in a domestic environment will often produce the same type of outlook in the youngsters from it. If they aren't taught or encouraged, to face their fears when young, then these fears will return later in life, and they will ill-prepared to deal with them. It is often ill prepared states that induce cowardice.

Jamie: If I was the most passive person on this planet - afraid of my own shadow, could I be converted into a tough guy, afraid of no one?

Dave T: *Converting a passive person to pacifism is usually dependent upon the motivation and rewards for it. Yes, I believe ANYONE can become less afraid by facing and controlling fears. The non-violent person will always have deep inside them a level that will bring their abilities to face fears to the front.*

In fact it often takes a 'tougher' man to walk away than it does to actually fight. If sticking to one's strong principles by non-engagement in violence is your way, and you stick to it, you are indeed a brave person. The problem with pacifism is that it can only work when both sides are in agreement. Pacifists often find themselves pleading for a non-violent solution to a problem, which though very laudable is often a 'feed' to another's aggression. Training can give us the edge.

Jamie: It can also give us the rank of Black belt. But does a Martial art Black belt mean someone is tough, if not - what does it mean?

Dave T: *A Black Belt is no more, no less than a degree of skill in a specific martial art.*

The ability to get it is usually a physical requirement.

It doesn't make you any tougher, only more skilful, unless you are with an instructor who fully understands fear control, and in most systems, this only comes in AFTER the Black Belt level.
In fact, in some situations achieving a Black Belt can give a false sense of abilities.

Jamie: Would you feel secure working a night-club door knowing that your colleague was a black belt?

Dave T: *I would rather have a doorman with a green belt, and many years door experience on my side in a real fight, than an untested 2nd Dan from a 'mild' system, who has never tested his/her fears.*

Jamie: Could you put all the tough guys you know of, into any sort of category? I.e. they are mostly from the forces, or mostly from broken homes etc.

Dave T: *It is not easy to categorise persons from sections as 'tough' people, and I think it's wrong to try. Experiences that allow people to face varying fears and control them are more* *determining factors than their social or geographical background.*

The armed forces prove this in the facts that it takes people from all walks of life, and can turn them into fighting units. But it's rarely as general as finding a category for them. So I don't like to do this. It's easy perhaps to say kids from a rough area will breed tougher people. But look at Audie Murphy, the American Film Star of the 50's. He looks 'soft', was turned down by the U.S. Marine Corps, for not being tough enough, joined the army, and became the most decorated soldier of the whole of World War 2.

Jamie: Some think that the Army makes people tough where as other feel that its a vehicle for tough guys to shine through and excel. Do you think that you can take somebody and make him or her tough? If not what is the nearest you can get them, to what you consider as being tough?

Dave T: *My answer to that is Yes, you can ALWAYS improve the level of anyone's abilities to face fears and be 'tougher', but if say on a scale on 1- 10, someone is only a 2 for example, and you add 5 to get him/her to a 7, he will still not have the same approach to violent confrontation, as say a natural 6 who becomes a 10.*

I know this sounds a little contrite and confusing, but it's the best way I can illustrate it. Tough in my book is the ability to stand up for one's beliefs, not back down from a one-to-one bully situation, have the courage of one's own convictions, confidence in one's abilities, yet tempered with the intelligence to know when NOT to engage in violence.

Jamie: As a young lad I had a pal, who many others and I considered to be the toughest person we had ever seen. He was a brilliant street fighter who was rarely defeated.
I met him 15 years later and he was a shadow of him former self flinching if anyone came near him in a threatening manner. It

was like his spirit had been broken. Do you think a tough guy can be made to be or become un-tough?

Dave T: *The example you mention has a myriad of possible root causes, it could be that he had become 'sickened' at his own level of violence, and simply didn't want to dish it our anymore. It could have been fear of retribution on his loved ones, a new baby for example. It was OK if there was a come back to himself, but not to his kids etc etc etc.*
I think EVERY 'tough' guy in time should mature to the level where violence sickens him because he now fully understands it. I feel it is natural progression from active participant to passive teacher. Yet 'un-tough' is a misnomer, in that we mature, not get softer, we look for the non-violent escape, not the ego - building punch up and defeat of our enemy. We have defeated our egos, thus we have less need to prove anything.

Jamie: Do you think it is possible to sense that someone is tough just from the way they carry themselves?

Dave T: *It is possible to sense toughness in others, but only for someone well seasoned in the violence scenes. A novice fighter will simply not be able to recognise the subtle signals, and will more than likely mis-interpret them anyway.*
Often the way someone carries themselves is a cover for fear, and in fact isn't a sign of toughness but of being unsure.
The man, who stays calm and quiet in the background, yet not showing fear is the one who has real strength.

Jamie: Is it possible to act tough without really being tough?
Dave T: *This is a natural follow on from your earlier question ... Just as it's possible to 'con' a novice into believing another's level of toughness, so it's also very possible to act the part. TALK THE TALK, BUT NOT WALK THE WALK... Dogs bark and growl, Gorillas beat their chests etc... This is no more than*

in built intimidatory actions... *Not only is it possible to act tough without being tough, it's natural and very common.*

Jamie: How would you deal with a tough guy who is in your face prompting you to kick off with him?

Dave T: *If I have already made the mistake of mis-reading this guy, and contrary to my teachings, allowed him to get in my face, I would trigger his own adrenal release by being outwardly aggressive myself, projecting my fear into aggression, pushing him away to give me the room and time to prepare myself for combat. If he stops where I have placed him and mouths off, I'll allow it, if I feel he is a further danger, then I will take him out without any second thought.*

Jamie: Is there a difference between men and women with regards to their toughness. I.e. would you be happy to let women take the place of men on the front line of pubs & clubs etc.?

Dave T: *Put simply, I feel women are tougher than men, but not as prone to having to prove it to their peers. I would have NO hesitation on allowing a well trained woman to be in the front line of anything with the massive proviso that they have been taught well, and tested their abilities.*

Jamie: Are you talking about training tough females the physical and thinking side of front line survival, or are you saying that you can toughen up a female to a level suitable for the front line, be it on a night-club door, gang fight, riot, etc.?

Dave T: *I don't actually think women in general need much in the way of 'toughening up'- A woman's mind is usually stronger than a mans. The protective instinct is very strong in most women. However, women need both the physical and mental training and testing, just as men do, before I would put them in the front line.*

The main problem lies in deep-rooted prejudice's regarding women and fighting. Yet women needn't lose their femininity to be good fighters. Throughout history women have proven to be fierce warriors once their training had given them the confidence to believe in themselves. A good modern individual example would be Sharon Thompson, Geoff's petite, but fierce wife. Sharon can both 'Walk the walk and talk the Talk' – yet is still a lovely lady.

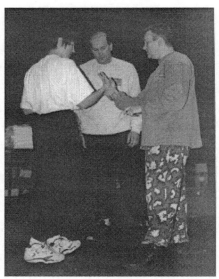

Jamie: Absolutely, you would certainly have your hands full with Sharon's capabilities. I suppose it's also helped that Geoff was Sharon's instructor. Private lessons from Geoff Thompson 24hrs a day has got to do something for you.

He knows his stuff and is very good at transferring that knowledge.

Dave, you also are very good at transferring your knowledge on self protection and the Martial arts, so I would like to ask you 'what do you feel the role of Martial arts has in making tough guys tough?'

Dave T: *God Jamie what a bloody question... It could and would take a full book to answer this one...*

The martial arts in themselves are not the answer to toughness... they are a tool or vehicle to achieve some form of mental toughness. As taught today in many clubs, they are next to useless. They give false impressions to the most impressionable...

Witness the would be bloody Ninjas.. The 'secret' killing arts etc. It's just Fantasy Island time.

A good Instructor who really understands the differences and joining of the terms 'MARTIAL' & 'ART' can help a novice reach the right levels of physical abilities and mental toughness. But unfortunately it's more often Pseudo- toughness that prevails.

On the less negative side, IF.. someone gains confidence, and IF someone has got increased fitness etc and IF someone understands that the street is far removed from the Dojo, and IF they know that most of their techniques are useless for a real fight, then OK I will concede that the Martial Arts have a role in making people tough. BUT A BLOODY SMALL ONE.

Some Martial sport arts, Judo for example, can test the practitioners to a greater extent than can Kata only competitors.

The aspect most noted by Geoff Thompson in his dealings with the 'Greats' is their humility and 'niceness.'

Real skilled tough men who know fear, strengths and weaknesses, and have conquered

ego, have little need for outward aggression..

Jamie: Dave thank you for your time in answering my questions, and the best of luck with your new full time martial arts studio in Rotherham and your columns in the Martial Arts magazines.

Dave T: *Thanks for asking me for my input, on this, your latest book, Jamie.. Glad to be of help.*
I'm pleased to see the direction your books are going, you are tackling many subjects that have not previously been sufficiently covered. Well done!

Mo Hussein
Former British Commonwealth
Boxing Champion

Jamie: Mo, if I was to ask you what you feel makes tough guys tough, what would your answer be?

Mo H: *My personal opinion would be – Whereas some people are born tough, I would say that upbringing environment has a lot to do with the moulding of ones character.*
I.e. Poverty, being bullied by people or older family, can all affect this. Growing up in built up areas where you constantly have to fight to earn respect from others or protecting a younger member of your family.

Jamie: I believe that anyone can go to a class and learn the Physical- Psychomotor side of an art and the problem solving-Cognitive side like 'what to do if X happens.' But I do not feel that you can learn the feelings - attitude - emotions - and values of Affective learning, which I believe can only come from life's experiences, making you what you are, be it tough or soft, bully or victim, etc. What is your view on this?

Mo H: *I have to agree with you on this point because it does not matter what fighting art you learn. There is no real way to apply certain techniques, unless you experience them under real conditions,*
Some things work for some people but those same things are not workable for others.

Jamie: If I was the most passive person on this planet - afraid of my own shadow, could I be converted into a tough guy, afraid of no one?

Mo H: *I think that some people can learn to be tough – but their level of toughness depends on their inner spirit, which can be translated as confidence.*

Jamie: You are well known for your Boxing ability, but you are also a competent martial artist and doorman.
So obviously you have had exposure to both boxers and martial arts practitioners of all levels. Does a Martial art Black belt, boxing title, or being a doorman mean someone is tough, if not - what do they represent?

Mo H: *I think with this question – my personal opinion, without trying to be prejudiced in any way, would be to categorise each one and break it down. I.e. Doorman, Boxer, Martial artist etc. Then look at them as individuals through one and another's experiences. To my knowledge, practising martial arts or Boxing at a competent level, or being a doorman, does not necessarily make that person tough - it merely represents that they are active within that field, be it, martial artist, boxer or doorman. Toughness would be classed by the individual.*

I would like to believe that a martial artist or boxer be categorised by the level of contact that they make during their respective roles.
Whether the come from doorwork, boxing or the martial arts, each of them have usually participated in some form of contact. Many doormen come from contact sports. Also any physical encounters they have on the door certainly involve contact.
You made reference to the term 'affective learning' as being the complimenting factor to which plays the all important role of making someone tough. I must say that with all systems - you have hit the nail on the head by using this wording. I definitely agree with you on the role of affective learning as nurturing us towards the end result of what we become in relation to toughness

Jamie: Could you put all the tough guys you know of, into any sort of category? I.e. they are mostly from the forces, or mostly from broken homes etc.

Mo H: *I would say that most of the guys, whom I would consider as tough, have mostly come from the working class, inner city type of people. Not always from broken homes, although sometimes this can contribute to how they end up.*

Jamie: Can you take somebody and make them tough? If not - what is the nearest you can get them, to what you consider as being tough?

Mo H: *I think you can always make them toughish, but the level of toughness that each individual will reach will depend on various things like which level they begin at when you take them on. If someone took me on as a student today they would be getting someone who has already had experiences from the street, boxing, martial arts and the door added to any upbringing that I personally experienced.*

Then compare this to someone who has had a comfortable childhood with no fights, no physical contact, no boxing, no martial arts, no doorwork, and this gives you something quite different to work with.

If the same bully was to pick on either of the examples with a full contact explosive confrontation based on each of our individual experiences and abilities, I think that you would see two different outcomes.

However given time, lets say the confrontation is a year away.

Then the inexperienced guy would be able to be trained in the practical and theory sides of self protection and will be more better equipped to deal with the situation. He could be toughened up.

Jamie: As a young lad I had a pal, who many others and I considered to be the toughest person we had ever known. He was a brilliant street fighter who was rarely defeated. I met him

15 years later and he was a shadow of him former self, practically flinching if anyone came near him in a threatening manner. It was like his spirit had been broken.

Do you think a tough guy can be made to be or become un-tough?

Mo H: *Yes*

Jamie: Do you think it is possible to sense that someone is tough just from the way they carry themselves?

Mo H: *Not always, but some people carry around them an aura of self-confidence.*

Jamie: Is it possible to act tough without really being tough?

Mo H: *Yes*

Jamie: How would you deal with a tough guy who is in your face prompting you to kick off with him?

Mo H: *Personally, I would always try to talk my way out. But if I felt at anytime that whilst talking, I was in any danger, I would act physically.*

Jamie: Is there a difference between men and women with regards to their toughness? I.e. would you be happy to let women take the place of men on the front line of pubs & clubs etc.?

Mo H: *Although spiritually, women may be as tough, if not tougher as men, I would think physically, it would not be possible. So No! I would not let them take the place of men on the front line of pubs and clubs.*

Jamie: What do you feel the role of Martial arts have in making you, or anyone tough?

Mo H: *Firstly, I would never consider myself as tough...I would rather say I was capable. I would consider most tough guys who blatantly consider themselves as tough, as really being bullies by nature. I have found this through experience but obviously this does not apply to all of them. I feel that if a person is already tough, the martial arts will then give them the ability to 'Know how' to take care of themselves in a more effective or efficient way.*
However if someone is already that way inclined, the martial arts would probably make no difference. But again it depends on the person's character.
I have seen many people practising martial arts, who may consider themselves as tough. But they are not living in the real world. If someone has ability, martial arts can give him the knowledge to be more dangerous or safe, Depending on which of the two they prefer or choose.
Jamie: Mo, we have been friends for many years now, going back to the old days in Canning Town. We have also spent time in each other's homes exchanging techniques and theory on self-protection, discussing the problems we each encounter working as doormen. I know that many of your door fights were all down

to you looking like the 'smallest doorman in the world,' as you would say. Do you think small guys are regarded as <u>not</u> being tough just because of their size?

Mo H: *Yes, some larger people would look at a smaller person and regard them as not being tough - We hear phrases used all the time like '**He is only a little fellow'** or the opposite to that from the smaller guy looking at his larger counterpart '**Look at the size of him, he must be able to take care of himself.'***
Many larger guys are able to hide behind their size whereas the smaller guy who gets picked on a lot through life and is forced to toughen up.

Jamie: When I first approached you about this interview, you instantly came back with 'I'm not tough.' You are one of the politest nicest guys I have ever known but you still take no nonsense from anyone who tries to take advantage of your passive nature.
I know that many people do regard you as a tough guy in the most respectful way. Do you think that toughness is maybe more in the eye of the beholder rather than the holder?

Mo H: *I would like to think that whilst most people who are regarded as tough - can be seen walking around oozing in confidence. They may not actually be aware of the fact that they are creating this affect on others.*
So I suppose it would be more in the eye of the beholder than viewed from the person themselves. You said that some people regard me as a tough guy, yet I certainly don't see myself in that way. I'm capable, but not tough.

Jamie: At what age did you begin boxing?
Mo H: *I was 14 when I took it up.*

Jamie: Can you tell me how long you boxed for and what you achieved?

Mo H: *I boxed as an amateur for 5 years then as a professional for 8 years. In my first year of boxing I won the Schoolboy title of Great Britain and went on to reach the finals at the National NABC. When I turned senior I won the London Divisional NE - I boxed for London against Kenya and Hungary.*

Jamie: At what age did you turn Professional?

Mo H: *At 19 years old.*

Jamie: How many fights did you have as a pro?

Mo H: *Thirty, winning 26 of them. Of the four I lost- two were on cuts, one on points and the other I was stopped, but still remained standing and didn't get stopped by being put on my back.*

Jamie: And you still regard yourself as <u>not</u> being tough?

Mo H: *That's right, again the word I prefer to use is 'capable.'*

Jamie: What other titles did you achieve?

Mo H: *As a professional I won the Southern area title and held the Commonwealth title.*

Jamie: What was your most memorial fight in boxing?

Mo H: *When I won the Commonwealth title by knocking out the champion in the last round of a 12 round war. He was a very experienced fighter, unbeaten by any British boxer prior to our fight.*

Jamie: Does your boxing ability naturally come into play when you encounter trouble as a doorman?

Mo H: *Working on the door, I have faced many situations and have obviously had the choice as to whether I used techniques from boxing or the martial arts.*

Thinking back, I probably favour the right cross and left hook from boxing because that's what comes naturally from 13 years of continuous use. I would then follow it up with a martial arts technique if the guy was still conscious and posing a threat.

Jamie: Can you give me a few examples where you have used boxing or martial arts in protecting yourself or others within your guise as a doorman.

Mo H: *This is not an area that I really wish to discuss for many reasons. One being that I do not want to come across to people that I am glorifying violence in any way, also I do not want to sound like I am trying to being some sort of tough guy.*
But anyone that works the doors in a rough environment will know exactly how it is and the reality of it is that problems do occur. So in this context I will answer your request reference actual events.
In your book Old school, New school, you included a section on **'who's behind you when its time to go home.'** *This brings to mind an incident that happened when I had left a club after work, to find three thug beating up a member of staff who they fell out with earlier. They were giving him a right kicking.*
I distracted their attention towards me, which served the purpose of saving the poor guy who was badly beaten on the floor. The three of them then decided to sort out the smallest doorman in the world - me!
I was forced into a position of having to defend myself.
My right cross put the first guy to sleep then I let go with a left hook to the second guy sprawling him over the top of a car, while the third man felt a jog coming on, and ran off.
I used the minimum force possible to deal with these guys and only used a pre-emptive strike when I was put into a position of fearing for my own safety.

Jamie: Its obvious here that your boxing experience played a major role in the outcome, can you give an example where you used only martial arts?

Mo H: *Yeah! One time a guy decided to shake my windpipe rather than my hand. As soon as he grabbed me around the throat, I introduced him to the martial arts by way of a rapid kick up the Niagara Falls. That quickly solved that one.*

Again I left it there and took it no further because the guy was no longer a threat to me.

It's just like being in the ring. Once you knock someone out you don't carry on and break their legs & arms. If you have stopped someone from continuing their physical attack on you-leave it at that.

Jamie: What about a combination of boxing and the martial arts working together?

Mo H: *We had to eject a couple of troublesome Skinheads from the club one night, who proceeded to stand at the door challenging all the doormen to a fight.*

They let it be known that their game was to beat up doormen in their hometown so we were no problem for them.

This happens everywhere to all doormen at some stage of their career, as you know. But the problem seems to strike a chord when they extent the insults to members of your family.

After 15 minutes of hurling abuse they began to bad mouth my wife whilst moving onto me in an aggressive threatening manner.

They crossed the safety line and met me at my breaking point. As the first guy went for me I let loose with a right cross-followed by left hook, which he managed to absorb with the help of alcohol, drugs and covering up.

We went into a clinch so I used a rear scoop from the martial arts to put him down.

Even after pinning him down, it still took a couple of right hands to put him to sleep.

Many people don't realise how much harder it is to put someone away that is boosted by alcohol or drugs but if I didn't knock him out he would have continued to try and seriously harm me.

Anyway the second guy is being held back by the other doorman but decides to pay me back for laying out his mate. He came at me but soon joined his friend. There are loads of incidents like on the door. You have had the same in the places you have worked, you know what its like. It would take a book to include everything that happens to you as a doorman. I'm surprised that you haven't written a book on this?

Jamie: I have, it is the first book that I ever wrote but still sits on my shelf.

Mo: *Why is that?*

Jamie: Because the good guys I have worked with are still within the security related field and I do not want to give out their personal information and tricks of the trade until they are happy for me to do so, and give me their approval.

The bad guys that I worked with would be put away if they were recognised from the book, plus I do not want to glorify them or violence in any way because they are just horrible people. In fact if you look through Old School - New School, you will not even find me talking about winning fights or beating people up. I have gone the complete opposite way in order to educate the good guys and cut out the bad guys. My whole life is based around dealing with bullies whether it be teaching female self-protection, releasing books, or working the doors.

Mo H: *So why did you bother to write the book if you are not ready to release it?*

Jamie: It got so much out of my system. Doorwork messed me up a little. It put my life totally out of sync with the rest of the world and changed me as a person for the worse. Tiredness is something that I didn't handle very well. I was snapping at my family for the slightest little thing, yet I was being nice to all the people that I met in doorwork who didn't give a toss about me. Writing about it made me realise how I was changing,
Anyway I may re-look at it and change a few names of people and places and this would enable me to publish it. I have partly done this with my book **'Thugs, Mugs and Violence'** which has plenty in it about my time on the door.

Mo H: *I would certainly look forward to reading it. I like your stuff and think that your other books are excellent.*

Jamie: Thank you for your comments, also many thanks for this interview which I know is hard after working on the door all night. Tiredness does funny things to our thinking so I know how hard it must have been answering some of these questions. Thank you for your time.....

(Since this interview was conducted I had been working with Mo for 3 years until an unfortunate incident occurred where Mo was attacked whilst working the door. This sadly resulted in the loss of life for one of the attackers and Mo being sentenced to four year imprisonment at the Old Bailey. The relevance in mentioning this incident is to clarify that Mo's answers in this book were years prior to and unconnected to this situation)

Bob Sykes.

Editor of Martial Arts Illustrated
5TH Dan Zanshin Karate
Former Full Contact Champion

Jamie: Bob, in your guise as editor as one of the country's leading martial arts magazine, you have come across literally every known name in the fighting arts, as well as the hundreds of lesser profile-seeking individuals.

Many of the people you have met are certainly regarded by many as tough guys, and some quite blatantly portray them selves as tough guys.
If I was to ask you what you feel makes a tough guy or makes tough guys tough, what would your answer be?

Bob S: *It all depends really on what your definition of a tough guy is. Mine is one who is well adapted at not falling apart during intense and stressful interludes of consciousness. One who doesn't hide from the truth, especially when it is the truth. An individual who is compatible at dealing with reality.*

Jamie: I believe that anyone can go to a class and learn the physical (psychomotor) side of an art and the problem solving (cognitive) side like `what to do if `X' happens'. But I do not feel that you can learn the feelings, attitude, emotions, and values of affective learning, which I believe can only come from life's experiences, making you what you are - be it tough or soft, bully or victim, etc.. What is your view on this?

Bob S: *Life can mould us in many different ways, all depending on your exposure to its many different experiences, be they physical, psychological or spiritual.*

Different people have different thresholds in dealing with these very varied spheres. For example someone who's maybe never lost a fight in the street or won one-hundred kickboxing bouts in the ring could quite easily fall to pieces or even spend the rest of their lives on medication, if they were to see a ghost or perhaps meet up with Rumplestiltskin in person.

Jamie: In your opinion, you being a teacher and exponent of the martial arts, if I was the most passive person on this planet - afraid of my own shadow, could I be converted into a tough guy, afraid of no-one?

Bob S: *No, due to experience being the best teacher, I don't feel that toughness can really be passed on from one individual to another verbally, especially the level of becoming both tough*

103

and afraid of no-one. That sort of toughness only comes via actual exposure. I could make someone believe they were tough, however that would be leading them into a false sense of security. An analogy I like to use is in reference to two cowboy films, 'The Magnificent Seven' and 'The Unforgiven.'
I don't know if you're familiar with the two films, but one focuses on the razzmatazz and gun-slinging magic, the other on having the guts to pull the trigger, watch both films and tell me what you think.

Jamie: That's a good example, and you are quite right in what you say. I think that the cowboy's gun can be compared to the martial artist black belt. The gun or the black belt represents the possibility of someone being capable of causing lots of damage. However the reality is that some black belts will go charging in like the magnificent seven and other will shake with fear when the storm breaks. Does a martial black belt mean someone is tough, if not - what does it mean?

Bob S: *Being a black belt doesn't necessarily qualify someone as being tough, instead it represents a level reached in one of the many different styles and systems available to the general public. In my mind, one has to travel a little further than their local sports centre if they really want to learn true martial arts.*

Jamie: True martial arts?

Bob S: *Yes, the real thing, the sort of stuff, which went out of fashion when fashion took over. The conditioning of the mind, body and spirit to such as extent that one could train a man to face the reality of death. That's what they had to do in Japan, How else could they persuade young men of the time to become kamikaze pilots.*
The samurai had to be able to let go of life, you can't grasp that if you're cashing cheques or chasing bits of plastic.

Jamie: Could you put all the tough guys you know of into any sort of category, i.e. they are mostly from the Forces, or mostly from broken homes, etc.?

Bob S: *Yes, people who've faced certain levels of adversity, but even they will have a chink in the armour somewhere or other.*

Jamie: Can you take somebody and make him or her tough? If not, what is the nearest you can get them to what you consider as being tough?

Bob S: *If they constantly train hard, pressure test and adapt a more realistic attitude then they would most certainly be moving in the right direction.*

Jamie: As a young lad I had a pal, who many others and I considered to be the toughest person we had ever seen. He was a brilliant street fighter who was rarely defeated.
I met him fifteen years later and he was a shadow of his former self, flinching if anyone came near him in a threatening manner. It was like his spirit had been broken. Do you think a tough guy can be made to be or become un-tough?

105

Bob S: *You can swim against the tide for only so long, eventually we all get crushed against the rocks. For some its a street confrontation, others a business going bust, or a mortgage repossession, even drink or drugs. I've seen many people fall victim to one or more of these elements.*

Jamie: Do you think it is possible to sense that someone is tough just from the way they carry themselves?

Bob S: *Body language says something about a person, sometimes though its a shield that they are hiding behind, other times they are the real mccoy. It's hard to tell, I look into the eyes, sense their aura, that sort of thing.*

Jamie: Does a kickboxing title mean you're tough, if not what does it mean?

Bob S: *Yes, in some ways, it certainly makes you more durable and encourages you to hit hard. It's also a good 'bottle' tester, it takes guts to get into the ring, it takes courage to turn a fight around especially when you've been knocked down a couple of times.*
It makes someone both mentally and physically stronger, however, to be honest, it is a completely different environment to the street.

In addition to all this, kickboxing doesn't really take grappling and wrestling into consideration.

Jamie: Are you tough?

Bob S: *No, I'm not.*

Jamie: What would you do if someone put themselves in your face right now, prompting you to kick off?

Bob S: *Although in my mind violence is an option, it need not necessarily be the only answer. I'd focus on verbal dissuasion while keeping my distance for the sniper option, that's a pre-emptive strike.*
I wouldn't at any time rule out the possibility of walking away.

Jamie: What 'rule of measure' would you use to measure toughness?

Bob S: *Well, not in feet and inches. There's an old saying where I come from which states 'there's many a big potato rotten.'*
I think that says quite a lot.

Jamie: Could you clearly define someone as 'not being tough?'

Bob S: *I wouldn't make that mistake. As you've said to me many times in the past, Jamie, and I quote your saying* **'anybody can do anybody, you just have to find a way .'**
Jamie: Can you give an example where you initially thought of someone as being tough, but their later actions or omissions led you to feel different about them?

Bob S: *Yes, but are we not all fallible within that department? Everyone swallows sometime or other, if we hadn't then we might not be here today.*

Jamie: Can you think of a time when someone that you would not normally regard as being tough, proved the case to be different?

Bob S: *When the bubble's burst I've witnessed green belts step in to help black belts who've been affected by the freeze syndrome.*

Jamie: Current technology allows us to buy books, videos, CD Roms and access internet sites that will sell us martial arts movements and problem solving philosophies to help us towards making an informed choice about self protection.
It has, sadly, even gone as far as 'Black Belts By Post' to satisfy those that cannot cut the mustard through the normal routes of learning and earning.
Do you think that it is or will ever be possible to buy toughness by mail order?

Bob S: *One can for any price purchase delusion; the thing about being deluded is you never know when you are. Things are getting easier, people in general are becoming softer, I sometimes feel as if we are being fattened up for the kill.*

Jamie: If that's the case, I think my times up. As for delusion, check out the Jodie Foster film 'Contact.' It deals with that very subject 'delusion' and also fear. What's your view regarding fear?

Bob S: Not to fear it, instead, try to indulge it.
Jamie: Bob, Thank you for your time.

Kevin Fox
Foreign Legion, T.A.s., Martial Arts, Security, Wrestling and Self Protection Exponent

Jamie: Kevin, if I was to ask you what you feel makes tough guys tough, what would your answer be?

Kevin F: *The psychological aspect is the most important – a persons mental strength and spirit. People talk about inheriting it genetically but I disagree with this opinion.*

Jamie: I believe that anyone can go to a martial arts class and learn the Physical (psychomotor) side of an art and the problem solving (Cognitive) side like 'what to do if X happens.' But I do not feel that you can learn the feelings - attitude - emotions - and values of Affective learning, which I believe can only come from life's experiences, making you what you are, be it tough or soft, bully or victim, etc. What is your view on this?

Kevin F: *I agree.*

Jamie: If I was the most passive person on this planet - afraid of my own shadow, could I be converted into a tough guy, afraid of no one?

Kevin F: *Under normal circumstances NO! However under very extreme conditions a normally passive person can be hardened emotionally and psychologically by the constant threat of death or injury. The 20-year-old college graduate who returns from Vietnam but cannot reintegrate into normal society again is a good example. They will have changed from the person that they were.*

Jamie: Changed in what way?

Kevin F: *The person becomes de-sensitised.*

Jamie: Kevin, I have always regarded you a bit of a tough guy having worked, trained and been friends with you for many years now. At times we have entrusted our lives to each other and I have always known that no matter how dangerous or heavy a situation has become. You would not, and never have let me down. What is it that makes you what you are, be it tough, hard, fearless, or what ever you want to call it?

Kevin F: *Basically state of mind, and inner confidence enhanced by training, practical knowledge and experience.*

Jamie: I can remember back to the times when we would go out in the middle of the night and grapple, lock, choke each other in car parks and other realistic surroundings to get that bit nearer to reality. We even used to train in a disused cemetery so that we could get stuck-in without prying eyes. These were the days when we both knew that grappling was vastly underrated by the martial arts world, opposed to now being flavour of the month. You went on to study grappling. Can you tell me if this changed you perception of tough, as you knew it in the martial arts?

Kevin F: *No! Wrestlers are like other fighters such as Thai boxers, who are striving to be the best they can within their training discipline. Naturally some individuals are tougher than others.*

Jamie: After we last worked together in the security field, you went off to train in the French Foreign Legion. Did this affect your opinion on what toughness is compared to being tough in the martial arts.

Kevin F: *You cannot compare the two. Warfare is life or death.*

Jamie: Having had a broad range of physical encounter in both the real world, Security, the Legion, the Territorial Army,

Martial arts, and in sport wrestling, which of all these areas of combat, do you think have contributed the most to you being tough?

Kevin F: *None of them – and perhaps a bit of all of them. The key is mental strength but you can improve your skills with knives, guns and grappling to increase self-confidence.*

Jamie: Could you put all the tough guys you know of, into any sort of category? I.e. they are mostly from the forces, or mostly from broken homes etc.

Kevin F: *No! It's down to the individual's strength, regardless of their background.*

Jamie: Can you take somebody and make him or her tough? If not what is the nearest you can get them, to what you consider as being tough?

Kevin F: *I've answered this in your third question. Only under extreme circumstances.*

Jamie: As a young lad I had a pal, who many others and I considered to be the toughest person we had ever known. He was a brilliant street fighter who was rarely defeated.
I met him 15 years later and he was a shadow of him former self, practically flinching if anyone came near him in a threatening manner. It was like his spirit had been broken. Do you think a tough guy can be made to be or become un-tough?

Kevin F: *What you didn't say was why he had changed? Presumably his spirit had been broken as he lacked confidence. His spirit does not necessarily have to be broken by a physical beating. Psychological problems could be just as destructive.*

Jamie: Do you think it is possible to sense that someone is tough just from the way they carry themselves?

Kevin F: *Not in all instances.*

Jamie: Is it possible to act tough without really being tough?

Kevin F: *Why not!*

Jamie: How would you deal with a tough guy who is in your face prompting you to kick off with him?

Kevin F: *Each situation is different, it depends on the circumstances?*

Jamie: Is there a difference between men and women with regards to their toughness. I.e. would you be happy to let women take the place of men on the front line of pubs & clubs etc.?

Kevin F: *No I would not be happy with that situation.*

Jamie: Why not?

Kevin F: *That is obvious!*

Jamie: What do you feel the role of the Legion or Territorial Army has in making tough guys tough?

Kevin F: *It can give a person the tools and ability to improve his self-confidence. The Foreign Legion. and T.A.s to a certain extent puts you in some very challenging situations both mentally and physically which again improves self-confidence.*

Jamie: Would you like to add anything on the subject of what makes tough guys tough?
Kevin F: *No!*
Jamie: Kevin, thank you for you time.

Peter Consterdine

Author of
The Modern Bodyguard- Fit to fight – Streetwise
Professional Bodyguard and Trainer
Karate 7th Dan
Chief Instructor of the British Combat Association

Jamie: Peter, If I was to ask you what you feel makes tough guys tough, what would your answer be?

Peter C: *I don't know! I don't think I have ever understood what tough means. In a fighting context do we mean someone who is a good technician and who can't be beaten or do we mean someone who is seemingly physically `hard' who can't be hurt, but who maybe has no technique. I say seemingly because often the hardness is just a 'front', which someone portrays simply to bluff others. As I can never come to terms with the definition I find it almost impossible to say what makes a 'tough' guy tough.*

I've been on the hills with good fighters who have folded under the physical and emotional stresses of carrying a heavy pack on their back for mile after mile. Often their toughness is 'state dependent' i.e they are tough only within a given environment, one in which they are comfortable and familiar and one in which possibly they have developed a reputation. Again though we swing back to tough as it applies to fighting. We probably need to widen the term to take in other conditions such as conditioning, resilience, strength, experience, and mental resolve.

I believe very few individuals are tough in the sense that they are resilient to pain and emotional stresses without training or conditioning.
There are individuals who are by birth 'hard men', but many, when you look at their development have, at some time, embarked on a road of learning which has made them confident,

113

resilient and most importantly focussed. Mental focus, that is the narrowing of attention to one singular goal, to the exclusion of all else, even pain and distress is probably the key to trained toughness.

Jamie: I believe that anyone can go to a class and learn the Physical -psychomotor side of an art and the Cognitive problem solving side, like 'what to do if X happens.' But I do not feel that you can learn the feelings - attitude - emotions - and values of Affective learning, which I believe can only come from life's experiences, making you what you are, be it tough or soft, bully or victim, etc. What are your views on this?

Peter C: *Life's experiences are personality shaping, but I don't agree that they are exclusively the answer to being tough. If that were the case we would simply be victims of our environment not masters of our emotions and ourselves. If a person is bullied it is simply an act of fate as to whether those experiences toughen him up or make him or her timid and afraid for the rest of his or her life.*
The individual at some point must be sufficiently inspired by circumstances to embark on a mental and or physical path, which makes them strong in both regards.
Deciding to embark on a martial arts path may be the catalyst and I believe that such systems can, not only imbue techniques, but very much effect a persons resilience, both to pain and to aggression. We become confused by 'tough' people primarily because we have a visual image of what we believe a tough person should look like.
If we had fifty people in a roam and asked them to describe their perception of how a 'tough' person should look they would probably all describe a very similar specimen.
None would describe someone like Reinhold Messner, mountaineer who was the first person, with a colleague, to climb Everest without oxygen, the first person to climb Everest solo

and the first person to solo all of the world's fourteen, 8,000 meter peaks.
My belief is that life's experiences have more potential to take the fight out of someone than it is to toughen them up.

Jamie: If I was the most passive person on this planet - afraid of my own shadow, could I be converted into a tough guy, afraid of no one?

Peter C: *It is possible to effect change in a persons attitude to life and himself. Self-image, confidence, self-belief are all deterrents to toughness if they are negative in someone. There is no question that with a hard and demanding physical training regime you can physically harden someone. They can be made stronger and fitter so that they would be physically resilient both to exertion and impact, but it wouldn't guarantee that they would become fearless men. The key, however, as we know, is not the physical attributes but rather the mental resolve and this is a very different matter. Making someone physically hard seldom has an equal effect on the persons mental resolve or focus although I believe it is the path towards it.*
For someone who is afraid of his own shadow the problem is one of confidence and self-belief. Affecting physical changes may be catalytic in changing attitudes, but not always. We should not always assume, though, that we need always change a person physically. It is possible to harden someone mentally without first hardening them physically. Again looking at people in challenging environments, I've taken people on the hills in very bad conditions, at night and with weight to carry and been amazed at who is more able to carry on. The fittest are not always the ones who can sustain the effort when, as they say, 'the going gets tough.' I've seen the hardest men crack under the emotional strain of the effort and pain.
Jamie: Some people seem to feel that becoming a black belt is the answer to being tough, Does a Martial art Black belt mean someone is tough, if not - what does it mean?

Peter C: *A martial arts black belt does indicate a certain toughness. This assumes that the system is reasonably physically demanding as is the grading system, but there must be some physical and mental toughness to be able to survive in the sport and pass a grading. If the question is meant to imply that by having a black belt one is 'tough' outside the Dojo then this is another matter. Most black belts are competent in handling confrontation in their familiar environment. Aggression, violence and the certainty of physical damage outside this, relatively, safe space can turn an experienced martial arts practitioner to jelly- I've seen it.*
This is why I started working the doors many years ago, because I knew that my martial abilities and myself had not been truly put to the test, even as a full Gt. Britain Karate International.

Jamie: So if being a black belt does not mean your tough! Can you put all the tough guys you know of, into any sort of category? I.e. they are mostly from the forces, or mostly from broken homes etc.

Peter C: *I don't know the answer to the question as to whether tough people are attracted to tough situations in the first place, or these environments, like the army, turn out tough people from any raw material. I know tough people from many backgrounds, military, sport, and others. There are some very specialised environments, which do produce more such people as we are describing than others. Certainly those Special Forces operations of armies around the world produce a soldier who will resist the rigours of pain, distress and discomfort far better than those produced by more average 'line' regiments.*
We know, however, that they need the correct material in the first place and that if that is not available they still cannot turn a pigs ear into what they require – hence the very rigorous selection procedures they apply to volunteer applicants. Such regiments do not attract people who do not have confidence in

their physical abilities at least, even if in the early stages of selection they find their mental resolve not all it should be.

Jamie: Can you take somebody and make him or her tough? If not what is the nearest you can get them, to what you consider as being tough?

Peter C: *A person needs some mental reserve to be 'tough.' It may be hard to find, but if it is not there no amount of physical training will make someone truly tough. Again I have a problem with the definition. Tough for what?*
I know people who are tough enough to run a 2-day mountain marathon and ignore the pain and suffering through mental focus.
These people are tough with a capital T, but they may back off from physical confrontation. The latter is unfamiliar territory and tilts a lance at their self-confidence. 2 months in a hard boxing gym, could, however, make a complete difference, because we know we have someone who is mentally able to deal with his emotions, even fear.
Many people I have who are tough are also stupid and this is the other category of those people who have little intellect, little imagination and, as a consequence, little fear or apprehension. To them most conflicts do not hold the terrors they might for other people.
I know these people and they are dangerous men. They may also have a low moral appreciation of the unacceptability of violence to others, which makes them act sooner than others in society may.

Jamie: As a young lad I had a pal, who many others and I considered to be the toughest person we had ever known. He was a brilliant street fighter who was rarely defeated. I met him 15 years later and he was a shadow of him former self, practically flinching if anyone came near him in a threatening manner. It was like his spirit had been broken. Do you think a tough guy can be made to be or become un-tough?

Peter C: *Anyone can have their spirit broken, assuming they had it in the first place. The case you mention may be the situation I described earlier where the individual perpetrated on everybody the ultimate bluff very early on. I know people who deep down are not tough, but who have learned to 'act' the part and get away with it. They face others down and with a few well chosen `cheap shots' continue to perpetrate the myth surrounding themselves.*

Jamie: Do you think it is possible to sense that someone is tough just from the way they carry themselves?

Peter C: *No. Some people can be described as confident in their personal manner and some people look tough as we said earlier, by means of most people's definition of how a 'tough' person should appear, but there are very tough people who you wouldn't give a second glance to. They may be physically unprepossessing, quiet and not particularly confident in social situations, yet turn them loose and they will need their heads cutting off the stop them.*
I know some very dangerous people who you would not look twice at in the street, but who have no conception of what loosing means, nor who would dream of giving up in a physically challenging situation, whatever the pain and discomfort.

Jamie: Is it possible to act tough without really being tough?

Peter C: *Yes, I've covered that in my last answer*

Jamie: How would you deal with a tough guy who is in your face prompting you to kick off with him?

Peter C: *I never consider myself as tough. I am physically resilient due to both physical and mental conditioning, but I am no different from, probably, the majority of people who when faced with overt violence would prefer to be elsewhere. I learned through many years of door work, though that not to act with confidence and correctness leads to a far greater price being paid, in mental terms than if I act to finish the conflict.*

I know that there are people I meet who will be superior fighters to me and who are tougher and as a consequence I cannot allow them to do what they do best - that's fight. Pre-emption is my only answer to being faced with imminent violence, but how to do it successfully is a book in itself (Streetwise may be a good idea!). I want it over quickly and I won't loose. I have made myself very good at what I do and I am able to keep control over my emotions and the array of chemical cocktails in the system.

It may be that I can psyche him out and with those whose toughness is an act it can work. With those to whom aggression is a permanent feature I may be less successful and to embark on this approach can have dangers. I also learned that taking that step into the problem is the greatest answer to any problem. I won't step back nor take `seconds' from someone, either verbally or aggressively. I make it `matter of fact' that I won't back down and often this can be enough.

Jamie: Do you feel that there is a difference between men and women with regards to their toughness. I.e. would you be happy to let women take the place of men on the front line of pubs & clubs etc.?

Peter C: *There are obvious physical differences in men and women, but little difference when it comes to mental toughness.*

119

In fact females are often more mentally resilient than men. The problem is with the approach to violence. Men are brought up in a more fighting inclined environment and violence is far closer to the surface in men than it is in women - generally! I feel that women working the doors are, in the right circumstances, a good thing. To believe that if a 16 stone violent man 'kicked off' that a 9 stone female would stop him is a myth, but when dealing with violent women then they are ideal.

Where a female door person is also invaluable is in ensuring that the 16 stone man doesn't 'kick off' in the first place. Women are more patient and can diffuse a potential situation better than most men, who may be personally challenged by aggression from another male and 'rise to the occasion.' The problem of women on the door is the same as women in the front line of armies in that a colleague may be more concerned for the safety of the female on the team in times of battle, than he is about attacking the enemy.

Jamie: What do you feel the role of Martial arts has in making tough guys tough?

Peter C: *Martial arts have a great role to play in toughening people up. The presumption has to be though that the system is physically demanding. I know from experience that if you are trying to keep students you will have very few if the training is hard.*

Not many people will subscribe to a continuing hard training regime and the 'rank and file' will seldom pay the price for better gains in the long term, in exchange for hard, rigorous and mentally demanding effort today.

I feel we often-loose sight of the 'martial' aspect of martial art. It is a practise of war and as such demands a certain price to be paid.

Some are prepared to pay this where many are not, but we know, fortunately, that not everyone can be a 'tough guy.'

Jamie: Peter, thank you for your time.

Micky Byrne
Survivor & Self Protection Instructor
3rd Dan New Breed Self Protection System

Jamie. Micky, in my opinion, the things you have been through in life far exceed any definition of toughness that I personally have encountered. For the readers, can you take us through some of the dramas that you have had, and tell me if you feel it has changed you in any way with regards to being tougher or softer.

Micky B: *I have had four major operations.*
A triple heart bypass in Nov 1983, a removal of a large Meningioma (Brain tumour) in 1993 and a second quadruple bypass in 1996, plus a full Heart transplant in March 1999, and I'm only 54 years old now.

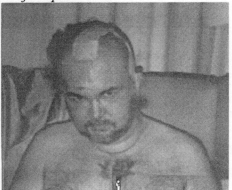

I have never considered myself a tough person, but a lucky person – to survive these dramas.

I am now mentally tough because anything the world throws at me couldn't exceed the physical pain and fear that I've encountered in the past.

Also having been a student of the New Breed self protection system as your student for the last 14 years, it has served me well with both theoretical and physical situations.

Jamie. If I were to ask you what you feel makes tough guys tough, what would your answer be?

Micky B: *There are two types of toughness, one is the toughness and sheer determination of the mind, to overcome physical or personal problems.*
The other is having the sense to realise that there is always someone out there tougher than you and to have the ability or toughness to just walk away.
You have always taught me that there is a big difference between someone hurting your pride and someone hurting your body.
If someone is hurting your body it takes physical toughness to deal with it, but if someone is hurting your pride - that takes a much stronger and different type of toughness. I'm still working on that one.

Jamie. Can you define at least one attribute that you would attach to a tough guy?

Micky B: *Self-confidence and common sense. But sometimes sadly, self-confidence blots out common sense. This can get you killed.*

Jamie. I believe that anyone can go to a class and learn the Physical -psychomotor side of an art and the cognitive problem solving side, like 'what to do if X happens.' But I do not feel that you can learn the feelings - attitude - emotions - and values of Affective learning, which I believe can only come from life's experiences, making you what you are, be it tough or soft, bully or victim, etc. What are your views on this?

Micky B: *I believe that a hard upbringing in the early years of a person, in the form of perhaps, lack of affection and being bullied does two things.*
It will make you show the world a tough exterior but you will be able to show others love and affection and that you care for them.

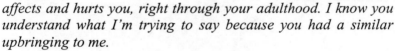

You will give them everything that you lacked as a child and do not want others to be denied the same things.

If you have been denied love and care in your upbringing - you will know how much this affects and hurts you, right through your adulthood. I know you understand what I'm trying to say because you had a similar upbringing to me.

Jamie. If I was the most passive person on this planet - afraid of my own shadow, could I be converted into a tough guy, afraid of no one?

Micky B: *Definitely not. You could learn a fighting art and gain ability in what to do in an encounter, which is why probably 90% of us take up the arts, but you cannot make someone fearless.*

Jamie. How are we to know when to choose 'fight or flight?'

Micky B: *Common sense comes into this. If yourself or loved ones are at risk of physical harm, and you have no means of escape, you will fight to survive just like a cornered animal.*

However if you are threatened with an edged weapon solely for the contents of your pockets, the casualty ward is the last place that you want to be, so I always suggest a quick exit wherever possible.

Jamie. Does a Martial art Black belt mean someone is tough, if not - what does it mean?

Micky B: *Not at all!*
It means you have taken the time with your efforts to climb the ladder to the top within that discipline, and should be able deal with situations should they arise.

I always compare this to my life as a musician - by constant practice I can, if needed, get out of tricky situations with a new band because I have underpinning knowledge and ability within music.

The same goes for dangerous situations in life where my martial arts knowledge and ability will help me out. Being a black belt should broaden your decision choice but certainly will not make you tough.

Jamie. Can you put all the tough guys you know of, into any sort of category? I.e. they are mostly from the forces, or mostly from broken homes etc.
Micky B: *I think kids from broken homes or sad upbringings become tougher than those in the forces.*
These types of children are toughened over time and it becomes the accepted way for them without them even realising it.

However the forces is a time served job where you have already experienced you basic make up of life experiences and they try to make you physically fitter and robotic through discipline. This is different to a lifetime of mental development that a hard upbringing will give you.

Jamie. Can you take somebody and make him or her tough? If not what is the nearest you can get them, to what you consider as being tough?

Micky B: *You cannot make a person tough if it is not in their makeup, but through training, they can develop an exterior attitude of being self confident or look tough in some peoples eyes.*

Jamie. As a young lad I had a pal, who many others and I considered to be the toughest person we had ever known. He was a brilliant street fighter who was rarely defeated. I met him 15 years later and he was a shadow of him former self, practically flinching if anyone came near him in a threatening manner. It was like his spirit had been broken. Do you think a tough guy can be made to be or become un-tough?

Micky B: *In some cases I think that it can happen. A person can loose their confidence through many things. E.g. If they become badly hurt in a fight, or mental breakdowns through personal problems. Even the loss of a job that they took great pride in. It depends on the particular person. All of these examples could also work in the opposite way and make someone even stronger.*

Jamie. Do you think it is possible to sense that someone is tough just from the way they carry themselves?

Micky B: *To see someone in the street dressed in something that would be considered as tough attire and acting in an assertive way, would give the impression that they are not the* *type of person to mess with, but in reality this may not be the case at all. Usually in close confrontation I would say that the eyes are the biggest give-away.*

Jamie. I know a documentary has just been made of your Heart transplant operation which is soon to be screened on television. However prior to this, I've seen you many times on the TV in programs like The Bill, East Enders, and like, playing the part of a tough guy quite a lot.
Forgetting your acting guise, in the real world, is it possible to act tough without really being tough?

Micky B: *Yes, but although you can fool some people some of the time, you cannot fool all people - all of the time.*

Experience of life allows you to differentiate the genuine article from a fake, in all walks of life

Jamie. How would you deal with a tough guy who is in your face prompting you to kick off with him?

Micky B: *I think this is best answered with honesty from past experience. Attack pre-emptively, Get in first without a doubt. You have always taught me that 'we only have one life to protect, if we get it wrong, we could lose it.'*
I value mine too much to give anyone the benefit of doubt.

Jamie. Is there a difference between men and women with regards to their toughness. I.e. would you be happy to let women take the place of men on the front line of pubs & clubs etc.?

Micky B: *Obviously women cannot be physically as strong as men, pound for pound, for those that wish to challenge that view, just go out to any area in any town and line up the first 100 males and 100 females you see and the evidence will show through.*

I do think though that they are equal in mental toughness.

Also I think that a female door supervisor would have more chance and ability to calm a situation be it a male or female problem but would still need the male backup if the situation escalated into violence.

Jamie. What do you feel the role of Martial arts, boxing, or other fighting related arts have in making tough guys tough?

Micky B: *A tough guy who has no training would come unstuck against an equally tough person with years of combat theory and physical training under their belt, be it from boxing, martial arts or wherever. Regular training will make a tough guy sharper and more confident.*

Jamie. Are you tough?

Micky B: *Not at all, but I'm not scared. Apart from my time recovering from my operations, I have spent 24 years training in self-protection and related arts, which has given me ability and confidence, but not toughness. If I am tough in any shape or form according to how you want to define it, its all down to my* *upbringing, lack of exposure to certain emotions, and experiencing the uglier side of life which was certainly lacking in the life's comforts that many people take for granted.*

Jamie: Micky, thank you for your time, and as always I wish you all the best with your future health.

Micky B: *Thank you.*

Buddie C
Vietnam Veteran - Marine
United States of America

The following interview has been cut short by my friend Buddie. Reason being that as we were going over the questions and I delved deeper into the subject of toughness in connection with the Vietnam War, it became a stained and emotional subject for him to talk about.

As with all the people I have interviewed, I promised that I would not put anything to print that the interviewee was unhappy with. With this interview I decided to put in the few questions that did not glorify the war or violence and also remain acceptable to Buddie. Many people in the U.K. do have a fascination or interest in the Vietnam War so I thought it best to include a few questions, rather than exclude it from the book because of its shortness.

I am off to the States for 3 week as Buddies guest so hope to conduct some more in-depth interviews whilst there to include in future publications.

Jamie: Buddie, as a veteran of the Vietnam War, toughness must have played a role somewhere with regards to survival. If I was to ask you what you feel makes a tough guy or makes tough guys tough, what would your answer be?

Buddie : *Vietnam is still a very emotional subject for me and I am not really able to face thinking about it very often, even thirty years later. This is very common among veterans as it is among people who have experienced something traumatic.*

I am not really up for airing any of my Vietnam experiences publicly, but will be happy to tell you what I think of toughness though. In the military, 'toughness' means discipline, training and leadership.

With good discipline and training a unit can be effective in carrying out its mission. In the traditional sense of the word, I don't think toughness enters in to it really. A well-trained and well-led unit can be relied upon to fight well and with a little luck perhaps be successful in battle. One thing that any veteran, particularly of Vietnam, will tell you is that any little fellow with a rifle can be just as tough as necessary. Bullets don't really care much about toughness.

Jamie: Buddie, you served as a marine in the Vietnam War. Without doubt you have had experiences that we in the United Kingdom can only ever grasp by watching TV. Forgetting about the politics of war, can you tell me what it feels like to be there in a true life or death situation were you have to be tough and are constantly fighting against your own emotions when forced to make a decision about life within a matter of seconds?

Buddie : *I think most servicemen would say that the reason they do what they do is because of their training and their desire not to let down their buddies. That is true until some other emotion affects you, then fear takes over at any rate.*

Jamie: Can you give me an example?

Buddie: *I was an artillery scout back in the days when you used a compass, a map and a radio. I clearly remember my first time under small arms fire. The whole issue for me was one of doing what I was supposed to do. I wanted to take cover and just lay there but I knew that the other guys would be returning fire and manoeuvring, so I reluctantly joined them.*

Jamie: What is it that drives you to follow them?

Buddie: *It's a matter of personal pride I guess. I was a Marine and we marines always have prided ourselves on our discipline under fire. The same is true of the English Army of course, after all Great Britain 'sets the world ablaze.'*

131

*It was because the Red Coats were disciplined enough to stay in
that line, fire and reload and fire again and advance, you know?
And the discipline comes from training and then loyalty to the
other soldiers.*
*But, there are all sorts of guys out there of course and you'd be
surprised at the things that happen.*

Jamie: Can you tell me about some of these things?

Buddie : *For instance there were about twenty Congressional
Medals of Honour, which is the American equivalent of the
Victoria Cross, awarded to Marines in Vietnam. Of all these-
only one I think went to someone who lived to tell the tale and
the great majority of the rest went to guys who did one thing---
they jumped on grenades. What in the world causes someone to
do that? It has to be a spur of the moment impulse because you
can also reach for it and throw it back, sometimes successfully.
They have a timed fuse on them and sometimes they just roll
around there for quite a while and everyone is able to get away.
Some of these guys must have grabbed the grenade and then had
a couple of moments to contemplate what they had just done.*
*It's a horrible thing to think about, really. But my point is that I
think they all did it for their buddies because we certainly
weren't trained to jump on grenades!*

Jamie: How do you feel about the Vietnam war now?

Buddie : *I have come to believe that the Vietnam thing was a
horrible tragedy for everyone involved, particularly the
Vietnamese, but that it was part of history and that it probably
contributed in a round about way to the downfall of the Soviet
Union because we were able to recover from all the turmoil and
come back and they just said, 'shit, we'll never beat these guys.'*

Jamie: Buddie, I realise how hard this interview must have been
for you. Thank you for allowing me to use some sections of it.

Roy Shaw
Prize fighter

Jamie: Roy if I were to ask you what you feel makes tough guys tough, what would your answer be?

Roy S: *Circumstances on the day, circumstances on their upbringing, circumstances on their way of life. For example I was bullied and circumstances forced me to deal with that. Then later in life I had the same from authorities and had to deal with that. I often*

get young kids write to me via my web site to ask me how to deal with bullying but it's not something that I can answer. How can I advise a young kid to go and smash someone's head in? Its what I think but I cannot write back to young kids and advise them to use violence so I end up not replying at all. It makes me feel sad for them because I was bullied and know what its like but I cannot be put in that situation where I'm advising young kids on what to do. My life was pretty unique due to circumstances and would not advise anybody to copy me.

Jamie: Can you define at least one attribute that you would attach to a tough guy?

Roy S: *That they can fight or are prepared to fight.*

Jamie: I believe that anyone can go to a class and learn the Physical side of an art and the thinking problem solving side, like 'what to do if X happens.' But I do not feel that you can learn the feelings - attitude - emotions - and values of Affective learning, which I believe can only come from life's experiences, making you what you are, be it tough or soft, bully or victim, etc. What are your views on this?

Roy S: *I think if you join in with some kind of group that get involved in fights then you will get the courage to have a go somewhere along the lines but I was a straight kid and wasn't involved with gangs or other groups of kids. My dad died when I was 10 which was a blow for me but it still didn't make me violent or anything like that. It was only after I was sixteen and became a hard working lad that circumstances changed things and I started robbing banks and getting in trouble with the police.*

Jamie: If I was the most passive person on this planet - afraid of my own shadow, could I be converted into a tough guy, afraid of no one?

Roy S: *I think it can work for some people who are not naturally tough. My grandson was only 10 when he was getting bullied so I took him down the gym to teach him how to fight. After going for about nine months he could punch the bag fairly hard and could lay someone out of his own size. He has surprised me, but he still didn't go out because he was frightened of getting bullied. He needed to build up his confidence. It was exactly the same for me. I lacked confidence even though as a kid I was physically capable of knocking people out. One day I just found that I was sticking up for myself against one of the bullies and from then on it all come together and I turned into Roy Shaw the hard B*****d somewhere along the line. Well that's the label that some people attached to me and not one I chose myself.*

Jamie: How are we to know when to choose 'fight or flight?'

Roy S: *The adrenaline rush chooses for you. Everytime I got the rush I would fight but some people decide to not fight when it comes. It left me alone for quite a while but recently I was in this* *club and there was this geezer who had raped a bird. I went over to him and there were these other two lumps with him but I didn't give a fuck. I liked myself up and let him know that I knew he was the one that had raped this girl and then knocked him spark out. I don't give a fuck if there are loads of them like when I did four of them, when I get that adrenaline rush; nothing is going to stop me. You know how it is you've done the same.*

Jamie: Does a Martial art Black belt or boxing title mean someone is tough, if not - what does it mean?

Roy S: *It means that they are tough as a boxer or martial artist and have the capabilities to use their art in a real situation but it doesn't mean that they automatically will. I've never done martial arts and to my knowledge never fought one so cannot really speak on their behalf.*

Jamie: Can you put all the tough guys you know of, into any sort of category? I.e. they are mostly from the forces, or mostly from broken homes etc.

Roy S: *I suppose the working class breed the majority of tough guys. You don't really see royalty or rich kids boxing. The Actor Micky Rouke was someone with money that could look after himself but he was like that before he become rich and famous. When I was in France he asked me to go to America and look after him when he was in his prime as an actor but it was not for me, I didn't fancy it.*

Jamie: Can you take somebody and make him or her tough? If not what is the nearest you can get them, to what you consider as being tough?

Roy S: *Well I'm a good example. When I left school at 15 I was quiet calm and only six stone one and had a history of being bullied. I took up boxing and soon realised that I had the gift of being able to punch and the aggression that I never had all seem to suddenly fall in place. I had a good trainer and that can* *really help you to develop. Even if a trainer hasn't got street fighting experience himself, he can still teach you and get the best from you if he understands and knows what he is talking about.*

Jamie: As a young lad I had a pal, who many others and I considered to be the toughest person we had ever known. He was a brilliant street fighter who was rarely defeated.
I met him 15 years later and he was a shadow of him former self, practically flinching if anyone came near him in a threatening manner. It was like his spirit had been broken. Do you think a tough guy can be made to be or become un-tough?

Roy S: *I've never known it! People mellow with age and mature but I've never seen someone who could have a row suddenly not be able to do it? Maybe a personality change is possible but it's not something I've come across. Having a family kind of controls you because you do not want to bring your aggro on their doorstep. I've got a mate who was a right rascal in his younger days but now he has got a couple of kids he doesn't even go out. He just cannot be bothered with the aggro but it doesn't change the fact that he is still capable; he just can't be bothered with it all. He has got more important things in his life now.*

Jamie: Do you think it is possible to sense that someone is tough just from the way they carry themselves?

Roy S: *Yeah, they have an aura about them that you can sense. People like us have got it. It attracts similar sorts of people towards you and that how you end up with a group of mates who can all handle themselves but it also attracts the mugs to you that wanna be tough.*

Jamie: Is it possible to act tough without really being tough?

Roy S: *not really, you can smell out a fake or plastic gangster a mile off. They don't kid anyone but themselves. A lot of mugs try* *it but they get caught out. You can only act tough for so long before someone will end up doing you.*

Jamie: How would you deal with a tough guy who is in your face prompting you to kick off with him?

Roy S: *I don't really get it happen to me these days. People seem to be more respectful because I'm not the kind of tear up merchant that I used to be. I'm more passive in my attitude when I go out these days. However if someone does try it on with me I will chose my reaction more wisely than I used to. I will still do then but I may bide my time to avoid witnesses and getting nicked. I had a situation at the country club last week. As I pulled up and stepped out of the cab there was a tear up going on and suddenly someone shouted 'Look out its Roy Shaw' then the whole thing broke up!*

Jamie: Is there a difference between men and women with regards to their toughness. I.e. would you be happy to let women take the place of men on the front line of pubs & clubs etc.?

Roy S: *No, women are not really fighting machines are they? I don't even like to see them in organised boxing events. Their bodies are not made up for being punched and that. The have got boobs and have babies. They are not made to fight like men, they are too delicate. Women are too be respected and not be beaten up or work the doors.*

Jamie: What do you feel the role of Martial arts, boxing, or other fighting related arts have in making tough guys tough?
Roy S: *It can help give people confidence. I did boxing so I would teach boxing to give someone confidence whereas you do it with the martial arts. I would probably teach martial arts as well had I ever studied it but I haven't.*

Jamie: Do you think that regional accents have any connection to toughness?

Roy S: *No not at all. Some regional accent like the East London or Scottish accent can make you sound tough but it means nothing.*

Jamie: Are you tough?

Roy S: *No but I can look after myself. A bit like you when you say that your not tough but you are capable, well I'm not tough but I can look after myself.*

Jamie: Does you current training system or method of training prepare you when confronted with a tough guy?

Roy S: *The boxing has made me the person that I am.*

Jamie: Is your current training system gearing you up towards toughness in any way?

Roy S: *Well I still do my weight as you know from the training session just now plus I do my running each morning with my dogs but my knees play up a bit now from all those years of power lifting, dead weights and squats.*

Jamie: Is there anything else you or anyone else can do to become tougher?

Roy S: *If you are a weak kid then you can spend time in the fighting arts training to become tougher. It will happen over a period of time if you persevere.*

Jamie: How many tough females can you name?

Roy S: *none. I don't really see females as tough; I see them as lovely human beings. I don't want to see them in any other way.*

Jamie: What do you think attracts people to villains, gangsters and fighters?

Roy S: *I don't think many people have got the arsehole to do a bank robbery or things like that or do the time in prison that goes with it when you get caught. Not many could go through Broadmoor like Frankie Frazier. People wished they could do the same but they can't.*

Jamie: Do villains exist today as they did back in the 60s ?

Roy S: *No, The Old School could have a row, stand up for themselves, had respect for each other, loyalty, all the things that make a good man. People are robbing each other in business and nicking cars and think they are gangsters. They are just paperback gangsters, wannabees. You cannot be the real McCoy without doing your apprenticeship. Knowing people that are gangsters does not make you one. You are what you are no matter what you tell people. Bit like that mug gangster that lived across the road to you old mum in Canning Town. He couldn't kid me, your mother or Frankie Frazier because we were all from the old school.*

Jamie: Is your life story going to be made into a film?

Roy S: *Well put it like this. We've been given £75,000 up front to give them the option for six months with another £100,00 to come on the first day of filming then 6% of the gross profits so I sure hope so. It's to be called 'Propoganda' and its being done by an American company. It looks like Ray Winstone is gonna play me in the film.*

Jamie: It goes without saying that you are one of the toughest guys in Britain regardless of if there are two, or two thousand tough guys. Are you able to control that anger that you once had or do you still explode? For instance if someone spilt your beer in a pub would you consider it something worth fighting for? Or if someone cut you up in a car in road rage?

Ans: *I wouldn't fight over a spilt beer but I did get cut up by a guy in a car outside my house the other week so I got out and*

139

knocked him out. I drove up the road after and sat for a while just to give him a chance to come round and piss off so no police were involved. When I come back to my house 20 minutes later he was still spark out slumped over the steering wheel of his van.

Jamie: I would give my life for my children. What would you be prepared to give your own life for?

Roy S: *I'd fight for my two dogs, my family, a friend or anyone who I knew was suffering.*

Jamie: We often hear it said that *'If anyone touches one of my kids I will kill them'* but the reality is that children do get harmed and killed but we don't see parents killing in revenge. Why do you think that is?

Roy S: *Because paedophiles move away and are untraceable. If they committed a crime against a kid and stayed living locally where people could get to them then they would not last long. We would do them inside the nick if we could get to them.*

Jamie: What would make you kill?

Roy S: *Next question.*

Jamie: What would you do if you saw somebody mugging an OAP or battering a child or animal.

Roy S: *Jump them and sort them out.*

Jamie:. Do you think that the journey travelled, pain suffered and life you have lost is worth the wealthy lifestyle you have now?

Roy S: *I wouldn't change anything but wouldn't advise anyone else to do what I've done because the cream years of my life are* *gone. But none of the screws that tried to make me suffer have the luxurious lifestyle that I have now.*

Jamie: Many youngsters and the not so young look up to you as a hero and role model that people can triumph over disaster. This is a big responsibility to bear because you are famous now and many people aspire to be like you, so how does that, make you feel?

Roy S: *I would turn youngsters against following in my footsteps. I lost my life from 27 to 37 and would not recommend that to anyone. All that I have today is from going into the gym and training hard, not from being a gangster.*

Jamie: Your website is coming along very well now. What do you think of it?

Roy S: *I've seen it but I don't really spend time looking at myself. I like your site.*

Jamie: Is there anything else that you still want to achieve before you retire?

Roy S: *No, I've done the book and I'm content with that.*

Jamie: What makes every day worthwhile to you?

Roy S: *Everyday is nice for me. I have a successful business, I love my dogs, and I train. Life is just nice. I love Mondays, which is when I collect the rent from my properties. What more could I want?*

Jamie: What is your stance on men that are violent towards women?

Roy S: *Any geezer that whacks a bird is an arsehole. I wouldn't even whack a guy who was drunk and incapable of fighting. I would go back and do him the next day.*

Jamie: What message or advice to young people who think it's cool to want to be a gangster or villain?

Roy S: *It's not cool. In the old days there were not the opportunities to earn money like you can now honestly. You can become a millionaire from making a computer programme, writing books and ways that you could not ever imagine when I was young. We had the choice of being hard up or going out and nicking a few quid here and there. Life is much better without crime. You can live a better life on the dole these days than you could get from grafting hard in the old days.*
These days I get my income from my lorry park, car site, my houses and my life story. Nothing could draw me into crime ever again.

Jamie: Is there anything you would like to add to this interview?

Roy S: *Thank you for coming to my home to interview me. I wish you lots of success with all your books and look forward to seeing you in Kate Krays new book 'Hard Bastards 2'.*

Richy Horsley
Streetfighter & Boxer/Trainer

Jamie: Richy, if I were to ask you what you feel makes tough guys tough, what would your answer be?

Richy H. *You can't make a guy tough. It is something that comes from within. It has to already be inside you.*

Jamie: Can you define at least one attribute that you would attach to a tough guy?

Richy H. *Someone who has proved them self to be tough in a certain situation.*

Jamie: I believe that anyone can go to a class and learn the Physical -psychomotor side of an art and the Cognitive problem solving side, like 'what to do if X happens.' But I do not feel that you can learn the feelings - attitude - emotions - and values of Affective learning, which I believe can only come from life's experiences, making you what you are, be it tough or soft, bully or victim, etc. What are your views on this?

Richy H. *Yes that's right. The real learning is done when you experience it for yourself.*

Jamie: If I was the most passive person on this planet - afraid of my own shadow, could I be converted into a tough guy, afraid of no one?

Richy H. *I don't think you could be converted into a person afraid of no one. But you could be made a lot stronger by learning to control your fear.*

Jamie: How are we to know when to choose 'fight or flight?'

Richy H. *Listen to your inner feelings. If they tell you things are not right and don't feel right then take flight and live to fight another day. I always reach inside to a quiet calm place and it tells me how to react. A sort of controlled aggression. Personally, I would never take flight myself even if I knew there was no way of winning. I'd go down fighting.*

Jamie: Does a Martial art Black belt or Boxing title mean someone is tough, if not - what does it mean?

Richy H. *You can't be a 'true' Martial Arts Black Belt or win a Boxing title if you are not tough. Black Belts and boxing titles should be earnt the hard way with full contact physical application being given and received as part of the achievement otherwise they are worthless and mean nothing. There has got to be a certain amount of toughness involved when these things have been earnt the right way. When you start Boxing and you start taking punches in the face, you either pack in or go back for more. To go back for more you have to be tougher than the average kid.*

Jamie: In your autobiography 'On the Chin' you tell of your journey from child to adult and of how your fists played a bit part of making you the person that you are today. Do you think that you could put all the tough guys you know of, into any sort of category? I.e. they are mostly from the forces, or mostly from broken homes etc.

Richy H. *All the toughest guys have always come from the working classes.*

Jamie: Can you take somebody and make him or her tough? If not what is the nearest you can get them, to what you consider as being tough?

Richy H. *My answer would be the same as question 4. I don't think you could be converted into a person afraid of no one. But you could be made a lot stronger by learning to control your fear.*

Jamie: As a young lad I had a pal, who many others and I considered to be the toughest person we had ever known. He was a brilliant street fighter who was rarely defeated.
I met him 15 years later and he was a shadow of him former self, practically flinching if anyone came near him in a threatening manner. It was like his spirit had been broken. Do you think a tough guy can be made to be or become un-tough?

Richy H. *I think there is still a little toughness there. I knew a few people when I was a kid who were hero worshiped because people thought they were so tough. As they became young men they were really 'fuck- all' and were getting bashed by mediocre people. That must really knock their plug in because you never heard of them fighting after that because they knew their limits. When you are young if someone tells you that a certain person is rock hard and one hell of a fighter you automatically believe them because when you are young you are vulnerable and believe anything.*

Jamie: Do you think it is possible to sense that someone is tough just from the way they carry themselves?

Richy H. *Yes. You know by instinct, you can sense it. They have an invisible aura. The non fighter may see lots of people as being tough but the fighter can sense out another capable person and also smell out a fake.*

Jamie: Is it possible to act tough without really being tough?

145

Richy H. *Yes, that's what Actors do don't they? I've seen it time after time. But when the heat is turned up, they always melt.*

Jamie: How would you deal with a tough guy who is in your face prompting you to kick off with him?

Richy H. *A few years ago I would have met fire with fire and would have given him what he wanted there and then. But now if there was no way of avoiding it I would take it elsewhere.*

Jamie: Is there a difference between men and women with regards to their toughness? I.e. would you be happy to let women take the place of men on the front line of pubs & clubs etc.?

Richy H. *No. Men are tougher fighting wise than what women will ever be. Women however are mentally tough.*

Jamie: What do you feel the role of Martial arts, boxing, or other fighting related arts have in making tough guys tough?

Richy H. *The rigours of the training make your body tough and there is also a mental side to Boxing, Martial Arts and other combat sports so it makes you mentally tough as well.*

Jamie: Do you think that regional accents have any connection to toughness?

Richy H. *No I don't.*

Jamie: Are you tough?

Richy H. *I would have to say no I'm not tough. Other people would disagree but I cringe when I hear people say 'He's Tough' or 'He's Hard'.*

Jamie: Does you current training system or method of training prepare you when confronted with a tough guy.

Richy H. *I am always prepared, even if I'm not training and haven't trained for a long time. I have lived and worked in that environment all my life.*

.

Jamie: Is your current training system gearing you up towards toughness in any way?

Richy H. *Doing the pads keeps me sharp, so probably yes.*

Jamie: Is there anything else you can do to become tougher?

Richy H. *You can prepare your mind to be mentally tougher. If you are mentally tough you will be tougher.*

Jamie: How many tough females can you name?

Richy H. *I know a couple of females who can fight like men and would beat some lesser men in a fight. Also some mothers who would find an unexplainable survival fighting instinct if their young were at risk but then again, I suppose we all find that courage when the need arises don't we? This is one of the natural occasions when we choose fight rather than flight.*

Richy, thank you for your time with answering these questions. I will let you get back to your training.

(Since this interview Richy has returned to the boxing ring and recently headlined at the Hammersmith Palis knocking his opponent out)

Your Chance to Answer

You have had the opportunity to read through, digest and compare the answers given by the people that I have interviewed.

My friend Dave Turton suggested to me that it would be good if the reader were given a chance to answer the same questions in order to make them think about the subject of what makes a tough guy tough. I have taken a selection of the basic questions to which you can add, edit or delete as necessary according to your place in life where toughness may be an issue.

It would have been good if the questions had been put to you before reading this book to see how your answers compared to those in this book, but obviously that was not possible. However now you can answer with a deeper insight on this subject.

It would be very interesting to see whether you current field directs you to answer and fall in line with the others in this book within the same or similar field to yourself, or will it have changed your mind in anyway about the route of learning that you have been pursuing. Maybe your opinion on what makes tough guys tough, will have drastically changed due to this exposure of a more informed choice. Perhaps it has made no difference at all!

Why don't you try using a cassette recorder and ask a friend to pose these questions to you so that your answers will come out in the way that you think.

Here we go!

Q1. If I were to ask you what you feel makes tough guys tough, what would your answer be?

Q2. Can you define at least one attribute that you would attach to a tough guy?

Q3. I believe that anyone can go to a class and learn the Physical -psychomotor side of an art and the Cognitive problem solving side, like 'what to do if X happens.' But I do not feel that you can learn the feelings - attitude - emotions - and values of Affective learning, which I believe can only come from life's experiences, making you what you are, be it tough or soft, bully or victim, etc. What are your views on this?

Q4. If I was the most passive person on this planet - afraid of my own shadow, could I be converted into a tough guy, afraid of no one?

Q5. How are we to know when to choose 'fight or flight?'

Q6. Does a Martial art Black belt mean someone is tough, if not - what does it mean?

Q7. Can you put all the tough guys you know of, into any sort of category? I.e. they are mostly from the forces, or mostly from broken homes etc.

Q8. Can you take somebody and make him or her tough? If not what is the nearest you can get them, to what you consider as being tough?

Q9. As a young lad I had a pal, who many others and I considered to be the toughest person we had ever known. He was a brilliant street fighter who was rarely defeated.

I met him 15 years later and he was a shadow of him former self, practically flinching if anyone came near him in a threatening manner. It was like his spirit had been broken. Do you think a tough guy can be made to be or become un-tough?

Q10. Do you think it is possible to sense that someone is tough just from the way they carry themselves?

Q11. Is it possible to act tough without really being tough?

Q12. How would you deal with a tough guy who is in your face prompting you to kick off with him?

Q13. Is there a difference between men and women with regards to their toughness. I.e. would you be happy to let women take the place of men on the front line of pubs & clubs etc.?

Q14. What do you feel the role of Martial arts, boxing, or other fighting related arts have in making tough guys tough?

Q15. Do you think that regional accents have any connection to toughness?

Q16. Are you tough?

Q17. Does you current training system or method of training prepare you when confronted with a tough guy.

Q18. Is your current training system gearing you up towards toughness in any way?

Q19. Is there anything else you can do to become tougher?

Q20. How many tough females can you name?

Affective learning within the evolution of female self protection

As a self-protection instructor, it has always puzzled me as to why I was bombarded with work in female secondary school, yet boys of the same age would not touch self-protection lessons within school with a barge pole.

It was always the case of 'I'm hard-I already know how to handle myself' or 'What can you teach me – I've had loads of fights.' Yet this never happened with the girls.

For years I had wondered why males felt that they were capable of protecting themselves, yet females preferred to take a different approach, accepting and requesting as much knowledge within this area as they could find.

Whilst training to be a teacher with Greenwich University I wrote many paper on areas of self protection but one comes to mind on this very subject which was an investigation into the effects of race, gender and discrimination on training programmes for Women's Self Protection.

This paper was called *'The evolution of female self protection'* which explored the route of affective learning within female self-protection.

You may think that anything on the subject of female self protection does not belong in a book that is essentially about **'Tough guys',** and that it would be better off published in my book **'Dogs don't know kung fu',** but the secret domain or hidden area of learning is in my opinion **'Affective learning'**, which is the major factor that comes into play in your final outcome.

So read what I have to say on affective learning within the evolution of female self protection, and hopefully you will have a more informed choice as to why men and women end up feeling different about their **'toughness,'** for want of a better word.

Here we go!

I had been teaching Self defence at Wimbledon high school for girls, for 5 year's prior to the murder of Rachel Nickel on Wimbledon Common in 1992. Although I had never taught or had any connection with Rachel Nickel, I decided to re-design my course, moving away from a physical techniques based programme to include more threat awareness, evaluation and avoidance of danger.

At the same time my daughter was born and brought a new perspective into my thinking.

I posed the question *'If I was preparing my own daughter to go out into the world containing rapist, murderers, perverts, stalkers, etc. What education and training do I think will serve her best to keep her from harm.'* From that day I have focused on Female self-protection and intended specialising in that area, So set out to identify and define the problem.

There are various ways that men have violated women's bodies but one of the ugliest fears has to be rape. So how are females protected by society.

The Sexual Offences Act 1956 simply declared that *'It is an offence for a man to rape a woman'*, (talk about stating the obvious) however this was not defined clearly and needed to be further amended in 1976.
It stated that a man commits rape if *'he has unlawful sexual intercourse with a woman who at the time of the intercourse does not consent to it; and at the time he knows that she does not consent to the intercourse or he is reckless as to whether she consents to it'* (**Butterworths Police Law**)

It is only within the last few years that forced Buggery also became classed as rape, which sadly seems to reflect the recent increase in male rape, rather than being introduced due to the abuse of women.

Prior to this females were sexually assaulted, buggered, and forced into oral sex, yet rape had not been committed unless sexual intercourse was forced, so a lesser charge of Sexual assault was used.

Rape is more to do with '**Power and control**' than anything to do with sexual desire. To explore this view further I spent hours chatting and reading about female abuse from males and discussing the rape aspect from the female point of view.

The collated information and views from this group were mainly directed to the idea that attackers are merely using sex as a weapon and that the potential rapist or sex killer is playing a power game, to show his power over his victim.

They are driven by a need to dominate submissive and compliant victims. Rape is essentially a crime of violence and domination, which includes a sexual element. Rapists derive their greatest satisfaction from terrorising their victims into submission.

To understand more about how training programmes are dealing with the concept of rape and female self protection in today's environment along with affective learning, we must take a look at female violation over time and see what measures have been taken to protect women from rape and other abuse from males.

This will help us to understand the affect it has had on their feelings, attitude, emotions and values, and obvious this will also apply to their male counterparts.

Environmental change and its effect on discrimination within female self protection, education & training

Primeval man became hunter, provider and defender of his domain when caves were their homes, dinosaurs were their wildlife, and survival of the strongest enabled their future.

The mould for feelings, attitude, emotions and values were being set and unbeknown to all, would stay the course of time.

Environmental conditions, individual choice, forced roles of gender, male dominance, application of power and control, plus many other factors may have contributed to the decision of which role the male and female took on.

I think that sexual desire and satisfaction would have been along the lines of animal instinct, taken as and when it's available. As far as we can understand, animals have no concept of Rape, so maybe the female at that time also accepted that there was no concept of rape.

I feel that the female's concern at that time would purely have been geared towards the protection of the home, the children, and the food supply. All available evidence of Stone-age cave drawings indicates that survival was the only thing of importance created by the need to eat. So the male created a Fighting method that would serve him as hunter and protector.

As time passed through the ages, our needs for self-protection changed. We formed methods of protection by training armies in a certain way according to the type of aggressor that we would face.

Whether naturally, or commanded, the trained armies of any country would mainly be male. As a result Protection of the people of our land and country became accepted by all as a male occupation, leaving the women to look after the homes and children, or make weapons of war.

This enforced the application of classification of roles by gender. I personally see this as a moral situation set up because men knew that they might die, and felt it in the children's interest to have the upbringing of their mother.

So the concept of rape still was not an issue that male society placed value on as a crime.

154

'In early recorded history, rape was a ritualistic way by which a wife could be obtained. Bride capture occurred when a man raped a woman and then was able to take her for his wife' History of rape 1996 - Women on the web.

It's quite clear that women were becoming regarded as property and the servants of man, which was now openly displaying discrimination and inequality.

I feel that a Sexist society was unknowingly created back with the caveman. Whether it was forced or happened naturally, it has become deeper and deeper inbred within all cultures, societies, countries, and individuals as the centuries passed.

Even when the Vikings went on their sprees of rape and pillaging, the focus for the female was on survival. Keeping themselves and children alive.

It is this time period that seems to be the first instance when **Rape was accepted in our minds as a crime that actually happens.**

This is possibly the reason the phrase ***Rape & Pillaging*** is remember-able, but protection against rape still remained unimportant compared to personal survival and protection of your young. Women were still being treated like trash, rape had become evident, yet ***Self Protection fighting systems still catered only for the male.***

Feudal Japans Samurai were feared world-wide but admired for their regulation of their own people and eradication of crime.
Women became servants to that society which imbedded discrimination even deeper into other's thinking.
The Japanese female became slave like, obeying every request without question, never speaking unless allowed to.
The concept of Rape and violation was not recognised by the male rulers although it did happen. No female was going to cry

rape for fear of being beheaded. Again there was no focus on a self-protection system for women, as it was, they were denied the right to protect their own body.

This extreme version of discrimination took men to a peak of tyranny over women who in turn had no quality of existence.

Self-defence or Martial arts.

The West were in awe Japans Martial art system of fighting and studied it throughout the 50s & 60s eventually watering the art down to a sport. Which again become male dominated and served the needs of men. It became an art that was studied for its own sake and passed on down the line strictly in its original form.

Men had no concept of the fear of being raped in traditional society unless they were institutionalised in borstals, prison etc. but reports of male rape and sexual assaults had always been evident in children's homes, boys boarding schools, and like, but in the outside world they would rarely expect or experience it, so the Martial Arts remained a field of study serving only the needs of men for the purpose of fighting but still no connection to rape prevention.

So from the beginning of time there has never been a true Self Protection system for women.

Suddenly the 60s had a revolution, which was to make a change for women on how they allowed themselves to be treated un-equally. The Contraceptive Pill became available!

This now this changed the feelings, attitude, emotions and values of many women - this was affective learning, about life.

Women now had control of when they became pregnant, if at all. At this level they had become mans equal.

Both sexes were now able to be sexually active when they want, with whom they want, with neither becoming pregnant.

The Scales of Equality had been balanced by technology.

This first achievement took around 25 million years.

In the mid 70s the Martial Arts boomed and T.V. now portrayed females fighting and defeating males using Martial art moves in programmes like Charlie's Angels, The Avengers, Wonderwoman, The bionic woman, etc.

This now opened the doors of Discrimination, Equality, and Gender in the World of Martial arts. Females were training in the Martial Arts just as they now do in Aerobics. They were training side by side with men.

At this point females had what they thought was a defence system against a rapist. Learning and applying the Martial Arts.

Reality

A deadlier, more ruthless, monster began roaming the streets in pursuit of women, to rape them. Nothing to do with the original male hunters acting on the principle of hunger and survival. It was now all down to power & control with a sexual element to it.

At a closer study it seems that some men now takes pleasure in the power and control that goes along with hunting, inflicting pain, torturing, and killing, just for personal pleasure. Whether it be Fox & hounds, Fishing, Pheasant shooting, Dog fighting, Male hunter raping and torturing woman, its all the same, Power and control..

Obviously not all men are like this but if a husband is legally guilty of rape, if his wife does not consent to intercourse, I feel that at some time through every long term relationship, almost every male will have violated his wife to some degree, so I think that in every male, the potential does exist.

What do I propose?

Throw the syllabus away and start from scratch. Don't take a male created art designed for use in Feudal Japan and try to apply it to a modern day rapist. Address the problem, as it exists now and teach Awareness.

To focus further on Awareness, Evaluation and Avoidance I would like to explain more about it.

Awareness:

You cannot possibly deal with any situation of danger that you may face in society unless you are made aware of the possible dangers that exist.

We begin teaching awareness of dangers to our children at a very early stage making them aware of strangers that may approach them. The dangers that may be associated with strangers such as being taken away.

Without this awareness the possibility exists of children innocently wandering off with a stranger totally unaware of the dangers that exist.

As they grow up we teach this awareness to our teenagers but from a more serious perspective quoting true-life case studies of rape, abduction and murder in order to raise their awareness. We now begin to educate the girls about awareness of relationships, parties, dangers of being attacked, the effects of alcohol and drugs etc. And all other problems they may encounter.

It becomes clear that a handful of motor fitness skills from the martial arts does not prepare any female for self-protection in today's environment.

If it did the papers would be full of Female Martial Arts success stories of how they defeated a rapist, but even up to present day there doesn't appear to be any.

All the victories have been in the favour of the rapist.

After around 20 years of martial arts not working for female self-protection in our society, they should realise that they are doing something wrong.

Female self protection education and training should focus on awareness of all dangers that they may encounter, evaluate the safest options for their safety, and then avoidance of the danger. Physical techniques are only taught to be used as a support system if the rest fails.

Changes I would like to see

I would like to see Female self-protection included into the Secondary curriculum as an option in year 10. This way a student would be able to take up self-protection as one of their 3 optional choices to add to their core subjects. This would allow me to define the application of knowledge skills as used in awareness, and re educate the pupils into this way of thinking.

The 6th form is another area I would like to establish the importance of Awareness, Evaluation, & Avoidance.

I feel that Female self-protection should be made available in Post Compulsory Education and Training because it is an ever-increasing area that continuously makes headline news. This shows that there is a need for education and training in this area if the problem has any hope of being addressed.

It is rare that any female will claim that they feel safe and confident in today's environment, and I feel that many would subscribe to a course of educational value that was structured and divorced from the idea of learning martial arts.
This programme would not at present be covered by Further Education Funding Council, which I feel maybe reinforces the low social importance given to violence against women. However it could become a full cost recovery unit as it is done in the Girls school.
My main difference in changing the way Self Protection will be taught is to teach in the classroom making use of Flip chart, Whiteboard, video, etc. and only visit the gym for the Psychomotor training.

This section on the evolution self protection should give you an insight into how male and female have ended up as a result of their affective learning.

So what is the answer?

Is it to put women out in the front line of pubs, clubs, and other violent areas of society? Is it to put women out to war whilst the men stay at home packing bullets?

Do you feel that the likes of Sadam Hussein would take a different approach to America's warning of possible invasion if he knew that the troops were to be female rather than male?

Can you remember how you felt in April 03 when the news showed the rescued 19 year old female American soldier - Jessica Lynch who was held captive by Iraqi forces? We saw the image of the broken boned "baby-faced" soldier lying on a stretcher in her combat gear. How did your affective learning experience that week compare to hers?

This gives us a lot to think about with regards to toughness, who is tough, and the route that we have to take in order to become tough.
It also makes each and every one of us ask ourselves why we are at the level of toughness that we are, be it plentiful, non-existent or somewhere in-between.

I put the question to you now.

Do you think that the male and female role in current society in relation to toughness could be any different or could have ended up any different if both genders took different routes of affective learning throughout evolution?

Have a think about it!

Conclusion

This book should give you plenty to think about in relation to what makes tough guys tough. I do not have all the answers but I certainly think that affective leering is a major, if not 'the' special ingredient that attributes to how you end up, be it tough or soft.

I believe that there is a point in our life where different stages of affective learning apply to the various guises that we take on in life.

My contributing factor of affective learning, which formed my attitude, may have been between the ages of 5 to 11 years old, whereas yours may have been between 8 to 20 years old.

It all depends on how we have accepted the way that others have treated us and our reaction to memories of that.

Children of a young age will walk into the path of an oncoming car or walk close to a cliff edge without giving any thought to the consequences towards their safety. This is because they have not had those particular experiences before.

We have to know what something feels like in order to decide if we want to experience that feeling again.

Could an un-sighted person ever experience the visual beauty of an attractive person on the T.V.? Or can a person without hearing ability, experience what its like to hear a seductive voice? There personal routes of affective learning would have been vastly different to many other people, however in turn, they will have travelled a different path of affective learning to others.

Anything that touches on our own feelings, attitude, emotions and values form our affective learning.

So the big question remains, can we nurture, tweak or fine-tune our affective learning to direct us and make us end up nearer to our ideal.

Maybe there are some things that we can change and possibly some that we can't.

I certainly feel that you can be conditioned to be either – Racist, Non-racist, Sexist, non-sexist, and like, but certain things like true sexual preference cannot be changed for you.

Now applying this to being tough. This I feel is an area in which you can definitely be conditioned towards. I do believe that you can be made tougher than you currently are or the level of toughness where you feel you are at, this moment in your life.

However exposure to environmental situations and scenarios are an important factor in strengthening this area.

You can work on the areas of feelings, attitude, emotions, and values of an infant from birth until X age and this will give them foundation from which to structure the rest of their lives experiences around. However to take a teenager who has already travelled a different path, and to then have someone else try to control their feelings, attitude, emotions and values – the result is going to be something quite different.

The path of affective learning has already been trodden. Changes can be made within certain areas, but some of these changes will not be vast.

Once into adulthood the challenge of changing or conditioning within the area of affective learning becomes even harder, if not near on impossible.

To give you an example:

As a 3 year old, you could have introduced me to the paddling pool, let me splash around, and sooner or later this would be a comfortable learning environment from which I could progress onto a swimmer, become a lifeguard, Scuba dive, and so on. Instead of that, my first exposure to the swimming pool was at secondary school level, when I was dragged fully clothed into the pool and held under water. Not quite the ideal first taster of an experience in the water. The end result being that, as an adult I cannot swim, remain petrified of water, and feel certain that's the reason I lost the part in Baywatch to David Hasselhoff.

I have no doubt that a good sympathetic coach could take me and help me conquer my fear of water and teach me to swim, but I will be hard work for them. Due to the fact that I am an adult conditioned to think in a certain way and act in a certain way, according to my affective learning. All I can 'stupidly and blindly' see is that if I jump in the deep end of the pool in my local swimming baths, I will drowned – simple as that. Logically, I know my chances of survival are much greater than my chances of drowning, but my feelings, attitude, and emotions tell me something different.

From my current level and abilities within water activities, I know I could improve to a certain degree. However if I were exposed to this area from infant-hood in a positive way, there would be major improvements in my ability and feelings as to how I feel within this environment.

My example of affective learning with swimming, at various stages in my life also applies to toughness, greed, hate, beliefs, preferences, and so on. We are **what we learn**, dictated by the **way in which we learn**.

I am not of the opinion that we are born tough, soft, etc.

Rather we are born with a level of physical and mental health, and abilities. Some better than average and some less than average, according to how we determine 'average.' Outside of that, I think we can all be conditioned towards literally thousands of different things, and being 'tough' is just one of them.

I feel that without doubt, that I could take an infant and put them through various experiences, exposing them to many different avenues of life conditioning then towards a desired end result.

This infant could be brought up to be Religious, Atheist, Racist, non-racist, devious, naive, and almost anything else you can think of. There feelings, attitude, emotions, and values just have to be fine tuned and directed towards the desired end result – so why not toughness as well!

The Greek philosopher Plato's, idealistic society would have seen children taken away from their parents at a young age to go and live out their childhood at Academy's of education.

He felt that the bonding of parent and child should not exist because this in turn would help rid society of greed, envy, jealousy, possessiveness, and so on. The children could then be conditioned along a certain path of learning similar to that of the

163

Shaolin monks, who took young boys into the temple along a particular structured route of affective learning.

Without the interference of input from parents passing on their own feelings, attitude, emotions and values to their own offspring's. The children basically had a clean state from which their guardians had to work from. They were carrying no baggage.

As adults we can go part way to improve within many areas that we choose to, however I firmly feel that some of out attributes cannot be changed, no matter how hard we try.

For instance, could Gandhi be turned into a bad guy, or a religious devotee be converted to atheism, or a gay person to heterosexual? You decide!

As individuals we can change some things about ourselves depending on how deeply rooted we are into where we have come from – and according to where we want to go!

Also the areas of change will be different for everybody.

I.e. You will never convince me in a million years that fire will not burn or damage my body, yet others can be convinced to walk across hot coals. This is an experience of affective learning, but I wonder how many of the same people will take a 2-minute bath in red-hot coals. The same can happen in relation to toughness.

Some people can be convinced that they have a certain level of toughness comparable to the few seconds worth of self-belief enabling them to walk the hot coals, but this bears no relation to real toughness.

Walking the coals or thinking tough for a few seconds is a false sense of security and far removed from actually being tough.

If you want to be tough, what is it that you actually want to be tough at?

Tough with customers, a tough fighter, a tough parent?

I assume from the basic theme of this book that its to be tough within the field of being able to survive and deal with confrontation at a level that you are happy with.

Take a look at someone who represents where and what it is that you want to be. Look as deep into their life as you can to try and find out the factors that contributed towards making them the person that they are.

If you only look at where they are now, be it a doorman, boxer, soldier, teacher, bully, etc. you will miss the all important route that they travelled in order to end up as they are. Don't blindly think that if you take on the guise of a doorman, boxer, martial artist etc that you will be of or automatically take on the same qualities and abilities of the person you admire or respect. It doesn't work like that. What you are seeing in them is an accumulation of continuous deposits and experiences towards their affective learning.

Richard Brandson is a good example to use. Many people can see no further than the image of a tough Multi-millionaire businessman who bought his own airline, but how many people know of the real path he took from his days as a student over 30 years ago.

Was Mike Tyson the tough aggressive fighter that we all see because of his boxing studies, or can you go further back to his childhood and see a path of affective learning within a learning environment that others have not experienced.

Another thing to consider is 'What if two infants were taken down the exact same path of learning, taught by the same methods, within the same learning environment – will they both end up the same?'

Well quite simply, the answer is no!

From the outside to an onlooker they may appear the same, but what they actually feel individually on the inside will be different.

There are many stories of two children being brought up exactly the same, travelling the same path in life, yet one ends up good and the other ends up bad.

It's all to do with something having an affect on their feelings, attitude, emotions and values.

There will be differences between the **biological and psychological** effect that each individual will experience when confronted with danger.

165

To teach a psychomotor skill, you can demonstrate a movement, which in turn can be copied and learnt as in the children's game 'Simon says.'

To teach using the cognitive method, you can present a problem, which the student needs to think about in order to supply an answer. However to teach via affective learning, the student has to actually **experience** an effect on their feelings, attitude, and emotions which coincides with their individual values.

Within a safe comfortable training or living environment where people do not feel what it's actually like to have certain experiences, it is not easy to create certain psychological and biological reactions.

We can go part way by taking part in full contact fighting, where we are going to feel higher and different levels of pain in connection with feeling scared. The adrenal rush is certainly the result of biological change taking place within our body. Over a period of time it becomes easier to deal with this inner chemical and mental condition. You could say that you were becoming 'tougher.'

When confronted with a real life or death choice, the biological and psychological effect on your feelings and emotions may be comparable to what you feel within your full contact art, but for others that life or death situation may multiply that feeling a thousand fold to an uncontrollable level.

Your Sport toughness may have equipped you well for true-life survival toughness but on the other hand it may not have equipped you in the slightest.

There is clearly different types of toughness that apply to different areas in life, which in turn are felt by each individual at different levels. So being tough in one area does not mean that we automatically qualify as being tough within another area in life.

If for the moment we replace the word '**Tough**' with a word I think represents the concept better, which is '**Capable**,' it will make it much easier for us to see ourselves and define areas within which we are tough.

I feel very 'Capable' in my ability to deal with confrontation in my guise as either a doorman or just on the streets if presented with a survival situation. However put me in the ring with a quality full contact fighter under rules and regulations – then I no longer class or see myself as 'Capable.' If you took that same full contact fighter and placed him on the front line of a rough night-club or in a true real life survival situation without rules, regulations and the medical safety net, their perception of 'Capable' may stay with them, but could also disappear.

Change the word 'Capable' back to 'Tough' again and you will be find all the areas of life within which you feel tough in, and obviously areas that you feel you are lacking in toughness. It's as simple as that!

We can all be the toughest kid on the block, **<u>depending on what our block is?</u>**

To my 4 children, I am the toughest kid on their block- that being my home. However if they take me to the local swimming pool, I am stripped of that title. I am not the toughest kid on that block. They each have had an affective learning experience that I have never had. I am the softest, wimpiest, un-toughest kid on that block.

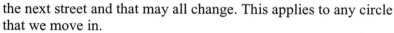

I might be a toughest guy down my street, but turn the corner into the next street and that may all change. This applies to any circle that we move in.

It is very easy to build our own pond and be the biggest toughest fish in that pond. We will always remain the toughest kid on that block if we do not let anyone enter it to threaten this position. Things will change though, when someone that we let in wants to reach or acquire your level of toughness.

You have the choice of evicting them from the pond, testing your toughness against theirs, using their level of toughness as your yard stick from which to raise or improve your personal level of toughness, or accepting them.

You may even move on and build another pond within which you can be the toughest kid on the block again rather that have your toughness challenged. You may even go on to join a bigger pond where you know or accept that you are not the toughest kid on the block.

There are many people that I know who would have their hands full if a physical confrontation were to happen between them and myself. But change the environment I.e. They drag me into the deep end of a swimming pool to fight me, things change.

I become the one with my hands full due to my fear of drowning.

This is a weak link in my chain!

The title of toughest kid on the block would change from me to him within no time at all. Forget all my years of training and all the fights I've had. My title has just been taken away from me.

I believe that **anybody can be done by anybody** – You just have to find the way.

I have come to the conclusion that we can all be tough, or capable (which I prefer to use), but that capability or toughness depends on where we position ourselves within the scheme of things. Put into a different environment and our level of toughness will lie somewhere in-between disappearing or increasing.

A 'tooled up' weapon welding gang member may have people shaking with fear and come can command that same effect on others who simply hear their name.

But transport that gang member into a similar environment where his name represents nothing and he has no reputation, he will be positioned somewhere else within the scheme of things in relation to toughness. Maybe higher – maybe lower. They may even decide to not enter that pool of toughness and set up their own pool elsewhere. Charles Manson was the toughest kid on his block, that being the 'Manson family,' but outside of that, for instance his position within the prison scheme of things are obviously different.

I can remember as a kid being treated like shit by another kid even younger than myself on a karate summer course for no other reason than his belt being black and mine being white. This lad genuinely believed that he was tough within the scheme of things that being that the 'Black belt' was though to represent toughness at the time. It was no fault of his own – he did not know any better. Taken out of that environment or pond, I could have taken him to pieces both physically and mentally. All of life is like that.

At the time I had fought almost every day of my schooling life compared to this poor lad who had never experienced a real confrontation outside of the non contact sport arena. He had a false sense of toughness, which sadly made him a bully.

I would like to wrap up by saying that I do hope that this book has made you think long and hard about the meaning and concept of being tough. Also where we fit into the scheme of things within different circles where toughness is an issue.

Plus how we can increase our own level of toughness from where it is – to where we want it to be.

I have decided not to write a conclusion on the interview section of this book myself. Reason being is that I would like you to write your own conclusion, which would include your own thoughts. You can compare all the answers that were given along with my thoughts and opinions on this subject, and your own answers to end up with your own conclusion based on informed choice. Try to give a reason as to why you have decided on a particular answer and give examples of at least one that you agree with along with one that you disagree with.

You may find that you end up with something worthy of a magazine article, or it could push you even further down the line to write your own book. If nothing else, I hope it has made you use your cognitive side in a way that you haven't used it before. Use it – or lose it!

Another way of looking at things!

For some people it is much easier to understand subject matter with the aid of pictures. A picture can paint a thousand words.

For the purpose of highlighting certain areas of the book that you may of missed, forgotten or not fully understood, I have enclosed the following photo gallery-linked to text in order to get your cognitive side working.

I hope this memory jog is of use to you when thinking about 'What makes tough guys tough.'

Does toughness feel different in unfamiliar surroundings?

Doormen continuously experience affective learning within their environmental workplace

What does a 'Black belt' mean to you?

Does toughness feel different when working alone?

The transferring and passing on of psychomotor skills

Brought together by a common interest, but
is it the pursuit of knowledge or toughness?

A good teacher will educate your brain as well as your body

Will imitating a psychomotor skill, make you tougher?

Driving is the perfect combination of Psychomotor, cognitive, and affective learning working in harmony with each other in its natural learning environment.

Is it important to look tough when doing personal security?

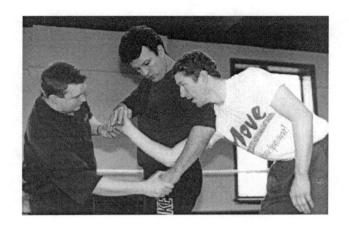

Martial art psychomotor movements can prove tricky for most people. Boxing does not naturally crossover

What does the Black belt award really indicate?

Why so few females? Is it anything to do with the evolution of female self-protection?

Should females replace men on the door of night-clubs?

Does the possibility of danger change your toughness?

Which one is not tough?

Same job – but difference in toughness?

Ugliness does not necessarily mean toughness!

Remember
Anybody can do anybody!
You just have to find a way
Jamie O'Keefe 1998

'Dogs don't know Kung Fu'
A guide to Female Self Protection
By Jamie O'Keefe **£14** including post & packing

Never before has Female Self Protection used this innovative approach to pose questions like. Why do Rapist's Rape? Why are Women abused? Why do Stalkers Stalk? This book takes a look at all Simple, Serious, and Life threatening aspects of Self Protection that concern us daily, along with **PREVENTION** of Child abuse and Child Abduction, Emotional cruelty, Telephone abuse, Road rage, Muggers, Date rape, Weapon attacks, Female abduction, Sexual Assault & Rape, Self defence law, and what it will allow us to do to protect ourselves, plus much more. With over 46,500 words, 77 pictures and 200 printed pages 'Dog's Don't Know Kung fu' is a no nonsense approach to women's self defence. It covers many realistic scenarios involving Children's abduction as well as typical attacks on women. Besides quoting actual events, the book explains how to avoid trouble and how you should react if you get into a situation.

**This book is a 'must read' for all women and parents.**

It is also important for teenage women, but, due to some of its graphic depiction's of certain incidences, parents should read it first and decide if it's suitable for their child.

Foreword

Dogs don't know kung fu

I'm not usually known for writing forewords to books on self protection, and not because I'm afraid of competition, on the contrary, the more people offering good advice in the fight for better protection be better:- rather its because most of what I read on the subject is crap.

I would never be happy putting my name to something that does not represent my own views, and that's putting it mildly. Not only are the proffered 'self defence' techniques in these manuals unlikely, they are also, very often, dangerous and opinionated.

I have written some 20 books to date on self protection and related subjects so you'd think that there would be very little left for me to learn. I rarely if ever find a manuscript that inspires me or even one that offers something new, a fresh perspective, an innovative approach.

Jamie's book did all the latter. He offered inspiration and sensible (and in retrospect, obvious) solutions to the many enigmatic 'grey areas' that had long perplexed me, a so called expert.

Questions that I have been pondering upon for years were answered at the first reading of this text. So I not only commend Mr O'Keefe on writing probably the best self protection book for women on the market but I also thank him for filling in the gaps in what is, at best, a very intangible subject.

What makes this book even more unique is that Jamie is a veteran instructor with thousands of hours of women's self protection under his belt, he is also an empiricist in that he has put his training to work in real life situations. Now while this may not say a lot to the lay man/woman, to those in the know, it speaks volumes.

Most of the instructors out there teaching self protection have never been in a real situation and so garnish unreal scenarios with un-workable, hypothetical technique.

You will get no such balderdash from this cutting edge instructor. What is offered on the menu in this text will prepare you, of that I have no doubt.

Self protection in the very violent 20th century must now, out of necessity be viewed as an environmental seat belt, it can no longer be down graded as a recreational pastime that comes third down the list of priorities after basket weaving, people are being attacked and killed, every day of the week, in un-provoked, un-solicited and bloody attacks.

My advice to you the reader is to take on board what Jamie has to offer as preventive measures and make them part of your life. Being aware will help you to avoid the majority of attack scenarios, for those that fall outside the periphery of avoidance, the simple, yet effective physical techniques on offer in this book will, if employed with conviction, help to neutralise even the most ardent of attackers.

This is a great book that makes great sense.

The best of its kind.

Geoff Thompson. Coventry 1996

BOUNCERS - SECURITY
DOOR SUPERVISORS
THIS IS THE BOOK THAT TELLS IT ALL

No matter what position you hold in
your workplace.
The actions of **Security**
will affect your safety and that of
the general public.

---

*Do you really know all you should
about
Door Supervisors?*

**Find out how much
Door supervisors
should know - but don't know!**
*If you want professionalism
from your Door Supervisors, you
must read this book*

If you want to become a Door Supervisor
You should read this book!
If you are a Door Supervisor, Security, or Bouncer,
You must have this book!
**No matter how long you have worked the doors – you will
learn something from this book**

*Peter Consterdine
Author of 'The Modern Bodyguard' said
'This book is a blueprint for the future'*

Foreword

Old School – New School

Whether you want to call them Bouncers, Doormen or Door Supervisors, they are still the people with the most thankless job I know.

Constantly under pressure from their own employers, local authorities, the police and especially the general public, it is no wonder that on occasions their self control is taxed to its ultimate. At times, even the best can lose that fine sense of perspective that allows them, night after night to take the constant barrage of banal and often alcohol influenced verbals whilst still keeping the smile in place.

I'd like to think that even going back some 23 years when I first started working on the doors that I subscribed to the "**new school**" approach so creativity described in Jamie's latest book. At that time I weighed eleven and a half stone at six foot one and despite having been on the Gt. Britain and England Karate Teams for some years I knew my traditional marital arts had limited value in the very particular conditions one finds in a night-club.

My weapons were politeness, humour, intellect and large doses of patience and, at times, even larger doses of pre-emptive strikes when occasion demanded. I'm the first to admit, however, that the conditions which applied in the seventies are different to today.

I saw the change begin in the eighties when, as a club owner, it was apparent that the nature of violence, the carrying of weapons, even handguns and the influence of drugs, was going to exact a heavy toll and so it has.

Twenty years ago when someone threatened to come back and shoot me, I slept easy knowing that the next day he wouldn't even remember where he had been the night before - now you'd be reaching for the ballistic vest.

Gang warfare, drugs, control of doors, protection rackets are all now part of the club scene and in the middle is today's doormen. Some are corrupt, some are vicious, some are plain thick, but the majority are honest, well intentioned and keen to do a good job in the face at mounting pressure from many quarters and increased violence and all this with "officialdom" now peering over their shoulder.

Often lied to by the police as to their correct rights of self defence under the law. This book should re-educate people about not only the law, but the many other complex issues.

Expected to be amateur psychologists and perfect man managers versed in a whole range of conflict resolution skills, doormen are still on the 'front line', both male and female.

Door licensing schemes are supposedly the answer to the problems inherent in the profession, but they only go part way to solving many of the issues which still give cause for concern.

Old School, New School clearly defines the gulf between the two approaches as to how the work should be carried out and it should be obligatory reading not only for all door people, but also the police and anyone who has an interest in the leisure industry. By doing so they will get a very clear and honest idea about the difficulties of this work.

Old School, New School isn't just a book about doorwork. It is an effective manual on modern methods of conflict resolution. Over the past few years there has been a substantial rise in the number of companies specialising in delivering courses on conflict resolution in the workplace.
If you read this book you will have all the answers to the management of conflict and aggression.
Doormen have been doing this for years, the only difference being the fact that they have developed their skills from intuition and experience of interpersonal skills in often very violent and aggressive environments.

Now we know that this is a science just as any other form of social interaction and **'Old School, New School'** sets out to educate on the complexities of what is required.

The book recognises, however, that learning these very specialised skills will still not be any guarantee that you can create a person who can be capable of operating in this increasingly dangerous environment. The job is harder now than it ever was and don't let anyone tell you otherwise. Doing this job puts you under a microscope and an official one at that. `Big Brother' most certainly watches over your shoulder and, many would submit, quite rightly so.

I know many doormen who should have no part to play in the industry and many people to whom the recent changes will be hard to adjust to. What I know for a certainty is that the inherent dangers of the work increase every year.

For those doormen and the people who control them to resist the pressure from others to become another drugs distribution outlet takes courage and confidence from everyone in the organisation. Many crumble and give in to the pressure and violence, but equally many don't and I hope that **Old School, New School** will give people not involved in this work, a clear insight for once, the dangers and complexity of the work. For those people who are in the thick of it, I believe that this book is a "blueprint" for the future.

Peter Consterdine

7th Dan Chief Instructor – British Combat Association

Author of :

The Modern Bodyguard

Fit to Fight

Streetwise

Pre-emptive strikes
for winning fights
'The alternative to grappling'

by
Jamie O'Keefe
£14 inc P&P
from
New Breed
PO BOX 2676, ROMFORD, ESSEX RM7 0LP

Foreword
Pre-Emptive Strikes

On first meeting Jamie O'Keefe, I was struck by his warmth and humour. I was then struck by his fists, head, & knees... Having been on the receiving end (though thankfully only in training) I can attest to the extreme effectiveness of the techniques he teaches. However, as I got to know him better, I was even more impressed by his integrity, honesty and commitment to teaching. Like many of the finest instructors and toughest fighters, Jamie is a gentleman.

These days I consider Jamie a good friend, but that's not why I agreed to write this forward. I believe he writes some of the best material available on modern self-protection, material, which can be, quite literally, life-saving. I am proud to be able to associate my name with such valuable work

So what is the value in devoting a whole book to the pre-emptive strike?

Be in no doubt that this is one of the most important concepts for personal protection you will ever learn. Over the years I have read about, trained with and worked the door with many individuals who have vast experience of real violence. Every single one of them *without exception* recommends and uses the pre-emptive strike as the prime tactic for self-protection when a physical assault seems inevitable.

This book thoroughly dissects the theory, training and practical application of the pre-emptive strategy. From legal and moral ramifications to pre-attack indicators, from action triggers to Jamie's unique 'Strike Storage & Retrieval System', this book is the most exhaustive, insightful and thought-provoking treatise on the subject I have yet seen.

The lessons contained within these pages were learned the hard way, with spilt, blood & broken bones - this book was written so you don't have to take that route.

Read, absorb, and live by Jamie's advice. You'll be stronger and safer for it. When talk fails and escape is impossible or impractical, the pre-emptive strike is your best option. I'll let Jamie tell you why.

Simon James Instructor, Close Quarter Combat Systems

THUGS MUGS AND VIOLENCE

Want to know what its like
when it really kicks off?

Forget the movies - this is the REAL world.

Jamie O'Keefe

www.newbreedbooks.co.uk

Thugs, mugs and violence
The story so far

In this true account of his journey, Jamie O'Keefe unveils the reality of living in the East End of London. From childhood to adult this compelling, harrowing and often highly amusing story tells of his encounters with streetfighting, crime, drugs, violence and the martial arts. It goes through the trials and tribulations of boyhood right through to his days of working on the door in the heart of London's nightlife. Read how each of his confrontations and experiences have played a major part in making him the well respected authority in the fighting arts that he is today.

This book is sure to intrigue and fascinate you so much it will be hard to put it down..

The names and places have been changed in order to protect the guilty

THUGS, MUGS and VIOLENCE

REVIEWED AS
'BOOK OF THE MONTH'
Front magazine

£14 inc p&p
from
NEW BREED
PO BOX 2676, ROMFORD, ESSEX RM7 0LP

The Late Reg Kray telephoned me from prison, after having just undergone eye surgery to talk through the foreword for the re-print of this book.

Due to time restraints and the restrictions that he is bound by, I asked him if he could sum up his thoughts, on this book in a lone paragraph, rather than a lengthy foreword. Although Reg has given me his consent to quote him in length on all the good things that he has said about this book. I have decided to just go with the lone paragraph which was written by Reg himself. *'Thugs mugs and violence'* now has a permanent place within the cell of Reg Kray and is also read by the other inmates.

Thank you Reg for you phone-calls, sometimes three a day, to share your thoughts, ideas, opinions and philosophies with me.

Your friend
Jamie

"Jamie's book 'Thugs, Mugs and Violence' is an insight into the violent times of today and should be read" **Reg Kray – Kray Twins**

Photograph kindly supplied to me for inclusion by Reg Kray

REG KRAY – 32 YEARS SERVED

1968 – 2000 HM Prison.

A NEW BOOK
AVAILABLE NOW

The latest book by Jamie O'Keefe

NO ONE FEARS
WHEN ANGRY!
The Psychology of
CONFRONTATION

Roy 'Pretty Boy' Shaw
And
Jamie O'Keefe
(Photo taken from book)

£14 inclusive of P&P

Elite Fighting System

The Home of Cage Rage

The Future of Martial Arts

www.elitefighting.co.uk

Highly recommended by Jamie O'Keefe